Oracle Certification Prep

Study Guide for

1Z0-050: Oracle Database 11g:

New Features for Administrators

Matthew Morris

Study Guide for Oracle Database 11g: New Features for Administrators (Exam 1Z0-050) Rev 1.4

Copyright @ 2012 by Matthew Morris. All rights reserved. Except as permitted under the Copyright Act of 1976, no part of this publication may be reproduced or distributed in any form or by any means, or stored in a database or retrieval system, without the prior written permission of the Author.

Oracle is a registered trademark of Oracle Corporation and/or its affiliates.

Information has been obtained by the Author from sources believed to be reliable. However, because of the possibility of human or mechanical error by the sources, Author, or others, Author does not guarantee to the accuracy, adequacy, or completeness of any information included in this work and is not responsible for any error or omissions or the results obtained from the use of such information.

Oracle Corporation does not make any representations or warranties as to the accuracy, adequacy, or completeness of any information included in this work and is not responsible for any errors or omissions or the results obtained from the use of such information.

ISBN-13: 978-1470168674
ISBN-10: 1470168677

Oracle Certification Prep

Study Guide for 1Z0-050

Table of Contents

What to expect from the test 9
What to Expect from this Study Guide 10
Additional Study Resources 11
Installation and Upgrade Enhancements 13
    Install Oracle 11g Part 1 13
    Install Oracle 11g Pt2 14
    Upgrade to Oracle 11g 15
    Oracle Direct NFS 17
    Use online patching 19
Storage Enhancements 20
    Setup ASM fast mirror resynch 20
    Scalability and performance changes 21
    Setup ASM disk group attributes 1 22
    Use various new manageability options 25
Intelligent Infrastructure 30
    Creating and using AWR baselines 30
    Setting AWR Baseline Metric Thresholds 32
    Control Automated Maintenance Tasks 33
    Database Resource Manager New Features 36
    Using new scheduler features 38
Performance Enhancements 42
    ADDM Enhancements 42
    Setup Automatic Memory Management 44

Enhancements in statistics collection 45

Partitioning and Storage Enhancements 49

Implement the new partitioning methods 49

Employ Data Compression 51

SQL Access Advisor Overview 52

SQL Access Advisor using PL/SQL 54

Using RMAN Enhancements 56

Managing Archive logs 56

Duplicating a Database 56

Back up large files in sections 58

Perform Archival Backups 58

Manage Recovery Catalogs 60

Create a Virtual Private Catalog 60

Using Flashback and Logminer 62

Overview of Flashback Data Archive 62

Manage Flashback Data Archive 63

Back-out transactions using Flashback 66

Working with Logminer 68

Diagnosability Enhancements 69

Setup Automatic Diagnostic Repository 69

Use Support Workbench 70

Run health checks 77

Use SQL Repair Advisor 80

Database Replay 82

Overview of Workload Capture 82

Using Workload capture and replay 83

- Using the Data Recovery Advisor 90
  - Overview of Data Recovery Advisor 90
  - Repairing data failures using DRA 91
  - Perform proactive health checks 93
- Security: New Features 95
  - Changes to Oracle Passwords 95
  - Encrypt a tablespace 98
  - Configure fine-grained access 99
- Oracle SecureFiles 103
  - Use Secure File LOBS to store documents 103
  - Use APIs to access Secure File LOBS 104
- Miscellaneous New Features 106
  - Enhanced online table redefinition 106
  - Enhanced finer grained dependencies 107
  - Use Enhanced DDL 107
  - Use Query and PL/SQL Result Cache 108
  - Adaptive Cursor Sharing 112
  - Temporary Tablespace Enhancements 113
- SQL Performance Analyzer 115
  - Overview of SQL Performance Analyzer 115
  - Using SQL Performance Analyzer 117
- SQL Plan Management 120
  - SQL Plan Baseline Architecture 120
  - Set up SQL Plan Baseline 122
  - Using SQL Plan Baseline 123
  - Automatic SQL Tuning 125

Setup and modify Automatic SQL Tuning 130

What to expect from the test

The test consists of 77 multiple choice or multiple answer questions. The passing score listed on Oracle Education at this time is 61%, but as with all OCP tests, they note it is subject to change. As with most certification tests, 1Z0-050 deals more with concepts and facts than with practical use. Assessing the ability to use features generally requires the test have a simulator to give the ability to enter commands or navigate a GUI. Oracle tests have never had a simulator aspect and show no signs of adding one any time soon.

When you sit to take the exam for 1Z0-050, you must understand what has been added or changed in the database with 11G, how that change affects using or administering the database, and the steps required to enable, disable, or configure the new feature. You won't be programming PL/SQL statements or navigating a GUI interface during the test. What is primarily being tested is whether or not you are aware of the existence of the new features and the purpose of the features.

That's not to say that you won't be required to answer any questions on how to use some of the new features. However, for features that are particularly complex to implement, you are unlikely to see a question that requires you to know the complete implementation process. Put another way, if a new feature is implemented with a single command -- you're likely to need to know that command for the test. If a feature requires thirty lines of PL/SQL to implement, you're likely to be asked a question about what the feature does rather than how to do it.

What to Expect from this Study Guide

This study guide will cover the majority of changes that were made to the Oracle database between the Oracle 10G and Oracle 11G releases. Oracle Education has a list of objectives for this exam, and this book has been designed to hit the knowledge areas indicated on that list. This guide assumes that you are already familiar with Oracle database as an administrator. The guide and the test are targeted for 10G-certified Oracle Certified Professional DBAs. You should have already taken and passed several exams showing that you have knowledge of the Oracle database.

This book is intended as much as possible to present information that is likely to be on the test at the level it will be presented on the test. As an example, for your career as an Oracle DBA, it would be ideal if you knew all of the PL/SQL procedures required to perform a SQL Performance Analyzer operation and could type them in freehand without referring to any manual. For the test, however, what is likely to be asked is the sequence of steps in analyzing SQL using SPA and possibly the names of the procedures used. There are other books available that are intended to teach you all of the details of how to use the new features of 11G.

Ideally in studying for any certification test, you should utilize multiple resources. One of those should be a source that provides the full details for using the new features. However, those tend to be hefty books that are hard enough to read through a single time. Read through them only once and you're liable to miss something important. This guide is small enough that you can read it several times before scheduling the test. Repetition will help to reinforce the knowledge and help prevent you from missing key facts that can lead to missed questions on the test.

Additional Study Resources

The companion website to this series is www.oraclecertificationprep.com. The site contains many additional resources that can be used to study for this exam (and others). From the entry page of the website, click on the 'Exams' button, and then select the link for this test. The Exam Details page contains links to the following information sources:

- Applicable Oracle documentation.
- Third-party books relevant to the exam.
- White papers and articles on Oracle Learning Library on topics covered in the exam.
- Articles on the Web that may be useful for the exam.

The website will <u>never</u> link to unauthorized content such as brain dumps or illegal content such as copyrighted material made available without the consent of the author. I cannot guarantee the accuracy of the content links. While I have located the data and scanned it to ensure that it is relevant to the given exam, I did not write it and have not proofread it from a technical standpoint. The material on the Oracle Learning Library is almost certain to be completely accurate and most of the other links come from highly popular Oracle support websites and are created by experienced Oracle professionals.

I recommend that you use more than one source of study materials whenever you are preparing for a certification. Reading information presented from multiple different viewpoints can help to give you a more complete picture of any given topic. The links on the website can help you to do this. Fully understanding the information covered in this certification is not just valuable so that getting a passing score is more likely – it will also help you in your career. I guarantee that in the long run, any knowledge you gain while studying for this certification will provide more benefit to you than any piece of paper or line on your resume.

Practice Questions

The guides in the Oracle Certification Prep series do not contain example questions. The format that they are designed around is not really compatible. The concise format used for the study guides means that adding a reasonable number of questions would nearly double the size of the guides themselves. However, because practice questions have been a common request from readers of my books, I have created a series of practice tests for the exams. The practice tests are available from the companion website listed in the previous section of this guide. They are not free, but the price is a fraction of that charged by other vendors for Oracle certification practice tests.

Unlike much of the material advertised online, these tests are not brain dumps. All of the tests are original content that I developed. Using these exams will not endanger your certification status with the Oracle certification program. I submit each test to the certification team after I finish developing it so that they can verify that they do not contain illicit material. These tests serve as an inexpensive means for any certification candidate that wants to determine how successful their preparation has been before scheduling the real exam.

As a purchaser of this study guide, you can use the following promotional code to get $2.00 off the purchase price of the practice exam for 1Z0-050: **050_IATYU.**

The tests are available at the following URL:

http://oraclecertificationprep.com/apex/f?p=OCPSG:Practice_Tests

Installation and Upgrade Enhancements

Install Oracle 11g Part 1

Changes to the OFA

The directory structure used in Oracle's installation process has been redesigned in 11G. The directory structure now centers around the ORACLE_BASE environment variable. Prior to 11G, setting this variable was optional and the only required environment variable was ORACLE_HOME. As of 11G, ORACLE_BASE is the only required parameter, and the ORACLE_HOME setting will be derived from ORACLE_BASE. The new structure streamlines how the installation is organized, and makes ongoing management easier. This feature improves manageability by making the directory structure more compliant with Optimal Flexible Architecture (OFA) specifications.

The default value for **ORACLE_BASE** is "**/mount_point/app/oracle_software_owner**". If you are installing as OS user **oracle** to the mount point **u01**, the default ORACLE_BASE would be: "**/u01/app/oracle/**". If the ORACLE_BASE environment variable is not set when prompted during the install process, the install will complete successfully, but when the database is started you'll receive an error in the alert log that ORACLE_BASE is not set in the environment.

Automatic Diagnostic Repository
The Automatic Diagnostic Repository (ADR) is a designated portion of the OFA directory structure for storing trace files and other diagnostic data. It provides a single location for all the serious errors encountered by the database and the data needed to diagnose and resolve them. The default ADR base directory is **$ORACLE_BASE/diag**. The default location can be changed with the use of the **diagnostic_dest** initialization parameter. The ADR structure is designed so that multiple database instances and other Oracle components such as Oracle Clusterware, Oracle OCI, Oracle Net, and more, can make use of the structure for storing diagnostic files. Each product has an ADR home using the syntax: **$ORACLE_BASE**

/product_type/product_id/instance_id. For an Oracle database with a SID and database name of 'orcl11g', the ADR home would be $ORACLE_BASE /rdbms/orcl11g/orcl11g.

Flash Recovery Area

In Oracle 11G, the Flash Recovery Area is located immediately below the ORACLE_BASE: **$ORACLE_BASE/flash_recovery_area**.

Data Files

The Oracle data file directory is likewise located immediately beneath the $ORACLE_BASE: **$ORACLE_BASE/oradata**. Note that Oracle strongly recommends you use separate physical drives for the oradata and flash_recovery_area directories.

Install Oracle 11g Pt2

New Components

Oracle has added several database components to the installation process.

- **Oracle Application Express** is now installed by default with Oracle Database 11g. It was previously available as a separate Companion CD component.
- **Oracle Configuration Manager** is a new optional component during installation. It was previously named Customer Configuration Repository (CCR). Oracle Configuration Manager gathers and stores details relating to the configuration of Oracle software.
- **Oracle Database Vault** is a new optional component during database installation.
- **Oracle Real Application Testing** is installed by default with the Enterprise Edition installation type of Oracle Database 11g.

- **Oracle SQL Developer** is installed by default with template-based database installations, such as General Purpose/Transaction Processing, and Data Warehousing.
- **Oracle Warehouse Builder** is installed by default with Oracle Database 11g.

Other Changes

- **Oracle HTTP Server** is now available on a separate media.
- **Oracle Ultra Search** is now integrated with the Oracle Database.
- **Oracle XML DB** is no longer an optional feature.

Upgrade to Oracle 11g

Upgrade path

An upgrade to Oracle 11G, performed either manually via scripts or using the Database Upgrade Assistant can only directly upgrade databases of version 9.2.0.4 or higher. Databases prior to that version must go through an intermediate upgrade process that results in a database of 9.2.0.4 (or higher) before you can upgrade to 11G.

Manual upgrade to 11G

When performing a manual upgrade to Oracle 11G, there are five scripts that must be run for the upgrade process to complete successfully. It's important that you remember function of each and the order in which they get run. When upgrading a database, the very <u>first</u> step is to make sure that you have a good backup. After taking a backup, you'll shut the database down and issue a **startup upgrade** to open the database in upgrade mode. Upgrade mode disables system triggers and prepares the data dictionary for update.

Once the database is started in upgrade mode, you can begin running the scripts. The Pre-Upgrade information tool is called **utlu111i.sql**. This script is technically a precursor to the upgrade. It generates a report that contains required and recommended changes that you must make. You might need to increase the size of SYSAUX, change or remove parameters, among other actions. Once the information tool indicates the database is ready, you will run the 11G Upgrade script: **catupgrd.sql**. This is the script that will make the actual changes to the database structure to bring it to the 11G model. If the script is stopped or fails before completion, it can be re-run multiple times. At completion, the catupgrd.sql script will shut the database down. Once it has completed, you will restart the database in normal mode and run the Post Upgrade Status script: **utlu111s.sql**. This script verifies that all components have been upgraded to 11G. If some have not, you will need to run the catupgrd.sql script again. Note that the Pre-Upgrade and Post-Upgrade scripts have very similar names. You need to remember which is which for the test. After the status script shows all components have been upgraded to 11G, you must run the Post upgrade actions script: **catuppst.sql**. This script is new with 11G and performs numerous upgrade tasks that don't require the database to be in upgrade mode. Simultaneously with catuppst.sql (or before or after), you may run the **utlrp.sql** script. This script recompiles and revalidates any database objects shown as INVALID in the Post-Upgrade Status script.

While it's not explicitly listed as a test component, I'll note that the script **catdwgrd.sql** is what you would use if you wanted to downgrade your database back to the pre-upgrade version.

Database Upgrade Assistant (DBUA)

It's also possible (and in most cases preferable) to upgrade to Oracle 11G using the Database Upgrade Assistant or DBUA. There's much less to remember (and much less to be tested on) with DBUA. You should know that DBUA can upgrade database and ASM instances simultaneously, whereas manual upgrades must upgrade them separately. DBUA is also somewhat faster at the end as it can recompile objects in parallel on multi-CPU systems.

The following enhancements have been added to DBUA:

- For single-instance databases, Oracle DBUA configuration utility enables you to upgrade from Oracle Database XE to Oracle Database 11g.
- You can move datafiles to ASM, OFS, or other storage devices, such as Storage Area Networks (SAN) and Network Area Storage (NAS), as part of the upgrade.
- The directory that you specify when you are prompted for ORACLE_BASE by Oracle Universal Installer is stored in the Oracle home inventory. DBUA uses this value to derive the default database locations and the DIAGNOSTIC_DEST parameter.
- The command line option AUTOEXTEND facilitates auto extending of the data files as a part of the upgrade. This option autoextends the data files during the upgrade and turns the autoextend back to its original settings after the upgrade.

COMPATIBLE parameter

The COMPATIBLE parameter of the Oracle database affects a great deal of its behavior. Much of the 11G functionality will be disabled if the parameter is lower than the database version. The default value for 11G Release 1 is 11.1.0. The default value for Release 2 is 11.2.0. For both R1 and R2, the minimum allowed value is 10.0.0.

Oracle Direct NFS

What is Direct NFS?

In 11G, a native NFS client capability is imbedded as part of the Oracle Database kernel. This feature improves performance and manageability when using Network File System drives. The Direct NFS Client improves I/O performance by incorporating Oracle-specific optimizations and eliminating the overhead from the operating system kernel NFS support. In addition, Direct NFS simplifies configuration by eliminating the need to manually tune most of the NFS parameters.

How to configure Direct NFS

To use Direct NFS, the NFS file systems must first be mounted and available via the operating system kernel. Direct NFS does *not* mount the drives. The specific mount options used by the operating system aren't important, as Direct NFS Client manages Oracle's access to the drive. The Direct NFS Client will use either a new configuration file called 'oranfstab' or the mount tab file (/etc/mtab on Linux) to determine the mount point settings for NFS storage devices. Oracle first looks for the mount settings in **$ORACLE_HOME/dbs/oranfstab**, which would specify the Direct NFS Client settings for a single database. Second, Oracle looks for settings in **/etc/oranfstab**, which specifies the NFS mounts available to all Oracle databases on that host. Finally, Oracle reads the mount tab file (**/etc/mtab** on Linux) to identify available NFS mounts. If duplicate entries exist in the configuration files, Direct NFS Client will use the first entry found. In addition to populating one of these files with the NFS mount settings, you must replace the standard Oracle Disk Manager (ODM) library with one that supports Direct NFS Client.

Sample oranfstab File

```
server: MyNFSServer1
path: 192.168.1.1
path: 192.168.1.2
path: 192.168.1.3
path: 192.168.1.4
export: /vol/oradata1 mount: /mnt/oradata1
```

Enabling the Direct NFS Client ODM Library

```
$ cd $ORACLE_HOME/lib
$ cp libodm11.so libodm11.so_stub
$ ln -s libnfsodm11.so libodm11.so
```

Use online patching

Traditional vs. Online Patches

Prior to 11G, all patches contained .o (object) files and/or .a (archive) libraries. Installing them required a relink of the RDBMS binary and therefore meant the database had to be shut down before the patch could be applied. With 11G, some patches are available as online patches. These contain .so files, which are dynamic/shared libraries, and they do not require a relink of the RDBMS binary. Because a relink is not needed, online patches can be applied or rolled back while the database instance is running. This simplifies administration, because no downtime is needed. It also means that installing or de-installing Online Patches is faster -- potentially taking just a few seconds. Online patches will be installed using the opatch utility.

Benefits

The benefits of online patches include the following:

- No downtime is required
- They persist across shutdowns
- They allow rolling patches in RAC
- They have a fast installation

Downsides

There are few downsides to online patches:

- They require more memory
- Online patching isn't available on all platforms
- Not all patches are available as hot patches

Storage Enhancements

Setup ASM fast mirror resynch

What is fast mirror resynch?

Fast mirror resynch is a new Automated Storage Management feature that allows a disk group to restore redundancy quickly after a transient disk failure. Using 10g ASM with disk group redundancy, if a disk cannot be accessed, it is taken offline and almost immediately dropped. To restore redundancy the mirror extent copies are resynchronized in the remaining drives of the disk group. This is an extremely costly operation.

Using ASM fast mirror resynch in 11G, if a transient disk failure occurs, the failed drive is automatically taken offline but it is **not** dropped until a predetermined period of time has expired. This time period is set by a new disk group attribute: DISK_REPAIR_TIME. During the time that the drive is offline, ASM tracks modified extents in the disk group. If access to the drive is restored before the drive is dropped, only the modified extents must be resynchronized. Restoring the redundancy is much faster using this process than the 10G model. Fast mirror resynch can only help when the drive failure is transient – a brief power loss, a loose cable, and so forth. If the drive fails such that there is a loss of data, or data corruption, fast mirror resynch cannot help.

DISK_REPAIR_TIME

The default value of the DISK_REPAIR_TIME attribute is 3.6 hours. You may change this by issuing the command:

```
ALTER DISKGROUP dgroupMain SET ATTRIBUTE
'disk_repair_time'='5h';
```

Note that if you provide a number for this attribute with no modifier, the default time increment is hours. You can also take drives offline and set the DISK_REPAIR_TIME if performing maintenance. The following example takes disk D2_001 offline and drops it after five minutes.

```
ALTER DISKGROUP dgroupMain OFFLINE DISK D2_001 DROP AFTER 5m;
```

Alternately, you can offline the disk and leave the drop time equal to the DISK_REPAIR_TIME attribute:

```
ALTER DISKGROUP dgroupMain OFFLINE DISK D2_001;
```

You can determine the current setting of the DISK_REPAIR_TIME attribute for the diskgroups in your ASM instance from the V$ASM_ATTRIBUTE view:

```
SELECT group_number, name, value
FROM   v$asm_attribute
WHERE  name='disk_repair_time';

GROUP_NUMBER NAME                     VALUE
------------ ------------------------ -----------
           1 disk_repair_time         3.6h
           2 disk_repair_time         3.6h
```

Scalability and performance changes

ASM Preferred Mirror Read

In Oracle 10g, if there were multiple failure groups, ASM would always reads the primary copy of the mirrored extent set. In a non-RAC database, or one where all nodes and failure groups are located at the same site, this behavior is not an issue. However, for an Oracle installation where there is a Real Application Cluster with failure groups and instances spread among two or more locations, it could cause significant network traffic. With Oracle 11g there is a new capability that allows each node to define a preferred failure group to read from. This would allow nodes in extended clusters to access drives from their local failure groups in preference to remote drives. This allows for faster access and lower impact to network bandwidth. The new **ASM_PREFERRED_READ_FAILURE_GROUPS** parameter is used to set the preferred failure groups for each node.

```
ALTER SYSTEM
SET   asm_preferred_read_failure_groups =
      'DGROUPA.DGROUPA_000', 'DGROUPB.DGROUPB_000';
```

Variable ASM Allocation Units

ASM files are stored in a disk group as a group of extents. In Oracle 10g a single extent mapped to a single allocation unit (AU) of a set size -- 1MB. The larger an ASM file gets, the more extents it has, and the more extent pointers are required in the SGA to describe the file. Oracle 11G reduces the number of extents required by ASM files in two ways. First, when you create a disk group in 11G, you can set the ASM Allocation Unit size to be between 1 MB and 64 MB in powers of two, such as, 1, 2, 4, 8, 16, 32, or 64. Larger AU sizes typically provide performance advantages for data warehouse applications that use large sequential reads. Second, in Oracle 11g the concept of variable size extents means that an extent can consist of one or more allocation units. The first 20,000 extents for a disk group will match the allocation unit size (1*AU). The next 20,000 extents will be made up of 8 allocation units (8*AU). Beyond that point, the extent size becomes 64 allocation units (64*AU). The combination of the two new features significantly reduces memory requirements for very large databases.

Setup ASM disk group attributes 1

ATTRIBUTE Clause

Oracle 11g ASM introduced the ATTRIBUTE clause to the CREATE DISKGROUP command. The new clause allows four new features of ASM disk groups to be configured: AU_SIZE, COMPATIBLE.ASM, COMPATIBLE.RDBMS, and DISK_REPAIR_TIME. I'll discuss each of these in turn.

Allocation Unit Size

As mentioned above, the allocation unit size of an ASM diskgroup is no longer limited to being one megabyte. In Oracle 11G, valid values for AU_SIZE are powers of 2 from 1M to 64M. This attribute can be set <u>only</u> during disk group creation; it cannot be modified with an ALTER DISKGROUP statement.

```
CREATE DISKGROUP dgroup1A
EXTERNAL REDUNDANCY
DISK '/dev/raw/raw1a'
ATTRIBUTE 'au_size' = '16M';
```

ASM Compatibility

The COMPATIBLE.ASM attribute controls the format of data structures for ASM metadata in the given disk group. The ASM software version must be equal or greater than this value in order to be able to access the disk group. The COMPATIBLE.ASM attribute must always be greater than or equal to COMPATIBLE.RDBMS for the same disk group. For example, you can set COMPATIBLE.ASM for the disk group to 11.0 and COMPATIBLE.RDBMS for the disk group to 10.1. In this case, the disk group can be managed only by ASM software with a version of 11.0 or higher. However, any database client of version 10.1 or higher can use the disk group. If you will be increasing both parameters, the COMPATIBLE.ASM value must be increased first.

```
ALTER DISKGROUP dgroup1A
SET ATTRIBUTE 'compatible.asm' = '11.2';
```

RDBMS Compatibility

The second of the compatibility attributes is COMPATIBLE.RDBMS. It dictates the format of messages that are exchanged between the Automatic Storage Management instance and the database instance. This parameter set the minimum database client release that may access a given disk group. You can set different values of this parameter on diskgroups within the same ASM instance for multiple database clients running at different compatibility settings. Note that the client database level is determined by the value of its own COMPATIBLE initialization parameter. A 10.1 database with a COMPATIBLE parameter value of 9.0.4 is effectively a 9.0.4 database from the standpoint of the ASM instance.

```
ALTER DISKGROUP dgroup1A
SET ATTRIBUTE  'compatible.rdbms' = '11.2';
```

When the database and ASM instances are using different software versions, the database instance supports ASM functionality of the earliest release in use. For example: A 10.1 database instance operating with an 11.1 ASM instance supports only ASM 10.1 features. Likewise, an 11.1 database instance operating with a 10.1 ASM instance supports only ASM 10.1 features.

Once either of the ASM compatible parameters for a diskgroup has been increased, it may not be set back to a lower level. You can find the compatibility levels of diskgroups in the V$ASM_DISKGROUP view:

```
SELECT group_number AS GN, name, compatibility,
       database_compatibility AS DATABASE_COMP
FROM   v$asm_diskgroup;

GN NAME          COMPATIBILITY    DATABASE_COMP
-- ----------    -------------    -------------
 1 DGROUP1A      11.1.0.0.0       11.1.0.0.0
```

Disk Repair Time

The DISK_REPAIR_TIME parameter determines the amount of time that a disk can be unavailable due to a transient failure before to being dropped permanently from the diskgroup. To use this parameter, both the compatible.rdbms and compatible.asm attributes must be set to at least 11.1. You cannot set this attribute when creating a disk group, but you can alter the DISK_REPAIR_TIME attribute in an ALTER DISKGROUP ... SET ATTRIBUTE statement to change the default value. If both compatible.rdbms and compatible.asm are set to at least 11.1, then the default is 3.6 hours. If either parameter is less than 11.1, the disk is dropped immediately if it becomes inaccessible. The time can be specified in units of minutes by using the letter M or hours by using the letter H. If you provide a number with no unit, then the default is hours. The default attribute value can be changed while bringing the disk offline by using an ALTER DISKGROUP ... DISK OFFLINE statement and the DROP AFTER clause. If a disk is taken offline using the current value of DISK_REPAIR_TIME, and the value of this attribute for the diskgroup is subsequently changed with the ALTER DISKGROUP ... SET ATTRIBUTE statement, then the changed value is used by ASM in determining when to drop the disk.

Use various new manageability options

Improvements to the check command

The ALTER DISKGROUP statement with the CHECK keyword allows you to check the internal consistency of disk group metadata. This functionality can check specific files in a disk group, specific disks in a diskgroup, all disks in a disk group, or specific failure groups within a disk group. In order to perform the check, the disk group must be in a mounted state. The CHECK DISK GROUP clause verifies all of the metadata directories by default. ASM will display summary errors and write error details in an alert log. The CHECK keyword will perform the following:

- Verify the consistency of the disk
- Cross check the file extent maps and allocation tables for consistency
- Check that the alias metadata directory and file directory are linked correctly
- Verify that the alias directory tree is linked correctly
- Check that ASM metadata directories do not have unreachable allocated blocks

In 10G, there were multiple options to the CHECK keyword to determine the extent of the diagnosis. In 11G, there are only two options to the CHECK keyword, REPAIR and NOREPAIR. This specifies whether or not ASM should attempt to repair errors that are found. The default is NOREPAIR which will provide you with alerts about inconsistencies and will prevent ASM from resolving the errors automatically.

```
ALTER DISKGROUP dgroup1A CHECK ALL;
```

Restricted mount mode

Oracle 11g provides a new option for mounting diskgroups called RESTRICTED. Mounting diskgroups in RESTRICTED mode will improve the performance of rebalance operations in a RAC environment. This option eliminates the requirement for lock and unlock extent map messaging that occurs between ASM instances. After the rebalance operation completes, the disk group must be dismounted then mounted in NORMAL mode. During the time that the diskgroup is mounted in RESTRICTED mode, it is not available to ASM clients by any of the Oracle instances, including the one it's mounted on.

```
ALTER DISKGROUP dgroup1A MOUNT RESTRICT;
```

FORCE option for DROP DISKGROUP

In 10G, when a serious error prevented a diskgroup from being mounted, it was not possible to drop the disk group directly. As of 11G, disk groups that can't be mounted by ASM can be dropped by using the new FORCE keyword of the DROP DISKGROUP command. This keyword clears the headers on the disk belonging to a disk group that cannot be mounted by the ASM instance.

```
DROP DISKGROUP dgroup1A FORCE INCLUDING CONTENTS;
```

SYSASM Privilege

Traditionally, storage management is the province of System Administrators, whereas managing the database is that of Database Administrators. With the introduction of ASM in 10G, either database administrators had to manage the storage, or system administrators needed SYSDBA access. In 11G, the new SYSASM operating system privilege and the OSASM operating system group allow storage responsibilities to be assigned to System Administrators without granting high-level access to the Oracle database itself. Users can be created in the ASM instance and granted the SYSASM privilege. This allows them to connect to the ASM instance and perform administration tasks. Similarly, assigning an operating system user to the OSASM group would allow then to connect as SYSASM using OS authentication.

```
$ export ORACLE_SID=+ASM
$ sqlplus / as sysasm

CREATE USER asm_admin IDENTIFIED by badpassword_nobiscuit;
User created.

SQL> GRANT SYSASM TO asm_admin;
```

Use md_backup, md_restore, and ASMCMD

The new ASM command-line utility (ASMCMD) allows ASM disk identification, disk bad block repair, and backup and restore operations of your ASM environment for faster recovery, among other capabilities. Two of the most important of the ASMCMD commands are md_backup and md_restore.

md_backup

The MD_BACKUP command creates a file containing the metadata for one or more disk groups. The backup file can be used to restore disk groups rapidly in the event of a catastrophic failure of the ASM instance. By default all the mounted disk groups are included in the backup file which is saved in the current working directory. If the name of the backup file is not specified, ASM names the file AMBR_BACKUP_INTERMEDIATE_FILE.

The syntax of the md_backup command is:

```
md_backup [-b location_of_backup] [-g dgname [-g dgname ...]]
```

Where:

-b Specifies the location in which you want to store the backup file
-g Specifies the disk group name to be backed up. Multiple diskgroups can be specified by repeating the –g option.

md_restore

MD_RESTORE is the complement to the MD_BACKUP command. It uses a previously created ASM metadata backup file to recreate diskgroups in an ASM instance. For the test, you particularly want to recognize the options for and differences between the three types of restore.

The syntax of the md_restore command is:

```
md_restore -b backup_file
```

-b Specified the backup_file.
-I Ignore errors. Normally, if md_restore encounters an error, it will stop.
-t Specifies the type of disk group to be created:
- full - Create disk group and restore metadata
- nodg - Restore metadata only.
- newdg - Create disk group with a different name and restore metadata; -o is required.

-f Write SQL commands to <sql_script_file> instead of executing them.
-g Select the disk groups to be restored. If left off, all disk groups will be restored.
-o Rename disk group old_diskgroup_name to new_diskgroup_name.

ASMCMD

The ASMCMD utility provides a suite of Unix-derived commands in which to access drives and diskgroups accessible to an ASM instance. Three of the most important are cp, lsdsk, and remap.

The **cp** command can copy files to or from

- ASM diskgroups on a single instance
- ASM diskgroups on local and remote instances
- An ASM diskgroup and the operating system

The **lsdsk** command lists the disks that are visible to ASM, using the V$ASM_DISK_STAT and V$ASM_DISK views. The V$ASM_DISK_STAT view is used by default. This command can run in connected or non-connected mode. The connected mode is always attempted first. The -i option forces the non-connected mode. Using the connected mode, ASMCMD uses dynamic views to retrieve disk information. Using the non-connected mode, ASMCMD scans disk headers to retrieve disk information.

-k flag generates detailed information
-p flag generates disk status
-s flag generates I/O statistics
-t flag generates repair information
-I prefix makes ASM retrieve data from file headers instead of V$ views
-d flag filters to a specific disk group

The **remap** command can remap disk sectors. It repairs a range of physical blocks on a disk. The remap command only repairs blocks that have read disk I/O errors. It does not repair blocks that contain corrupted contents, whether or not those blocks can be read.

Intelligent Infrastructure

Creating and using AWR baselines

System-defined moving window baseline

An Oracle baseline contains performance data from a specific time period. It's used for comparison with other similar workload periods to troubleshoot performance problems. AWR snapshots in a baseline are excluded from the automatic purging process and are retained indefinitely.

- A fixed baseline corresponds to a fixed, contiguous time period in the past.
- A moving window baseline uses all of the data in the AWR retention period.
- A baseline template allows you to create baselines for a time period in the future.

Fixed baselines are useful for tracking performance changes over extended periods of time. Moving window baselines are useful when using adaptive thresholds because the data in the entire AWR retention period can be used to compute threshold values. Oracle automatically maintains a system-defined moving window baseline. The default window size for the system-defined moving window baseline is the current AWR retention period, which by default is 8 days. Consider using a larger moving window—such as 30 days if you are planning to use adaptive thresholds. A larger period will more accurately compute threshold values. To increase the size of a moving window, you must first increase the AWR retention period. In order to make use of thresholds, the baseline window size must be eight days or greater.

```
BEGIN
  DBMS_WORKLOAD_REPOSITORY.MODIFY_BASELINE_WINDOW_SIZE (
     window_size => 14);
END;
```

AWR Baseline Enhancements

Baseline templates schedule a baseline to be created for a contiguous time period in the future. It's possible to create single and repeating baseline templates.

A single baseline template is used to create a baseline for a single contiguous time period in the future. They can be used if you know of an event in the future that you want to capture metrics for. A repeating baseline template is used to create and drop baselines on a repeating schedule. This is used when you want Oracle to capture a contiguous time period multiple times.

There are two types of adaptive thresholds:

- **Percentage of maximum:** The threshold value is computed as a percentage multiple of the maximum value observed for the data in the moving window baseline.
- **Significance level**: The threshold value is set to a statistical percentile that represents how unusual it is to observe values above the threshold value based the data in the moving window baseline. The significance levels are:
  - ✓ High (.95): Only 5 in 100 observations are expected to exceed this value.
  - ✓ Very High (.99): Only 1 in 100 observations are expected to exceed this value.
  - ✓ Severe (.999): Only 1 in 1,000 observations are expected to exceed this value.
  - ✓ Extreme (.9999): Only 1 in 10,000 observations are expected to exceed this value.

There are several new procedures in DBMS_WORKLOAD_REPOSITORY to support the baseline functionality.

- **CREATE_BASELINE**: Creates a single baseline
- **CREATE_BASELINE_TEMPLATE**: Creates a baseline template
- **DROP_BASELINE**: Drops a range of snapshots
- **DROP_BASELINE_TEMPLATE**: Removes a baseline template that is no longer needed
- **MODIFY_BASELINE_WINDOW_SIZE**: Modifies the size for the Default Moving Window Baseline
- **RENAME_BASELINE**: Renames a baseline
- **SELECT_BASELINE_METRICS**: Shows the values of the metrics corresponding to a baseline

Setting AWR Baseline Metric Thresholds

Oracle Enterprise Manager is used to set baseline metric thresholds. Without a simulator the steps for this process from a testing standpoint are meaningless. You need to understand how the four Threshold settings apply to baselines.

- **Threshold Type** – Can be Percentage of Maximum or Significance Level.
- **Critical** – If the type is Percentage of Maximum, this would be set to a percentage. Otherwise, it would be one of the significance levels (High, Very High, Severe, Extreme).
- **Warning** – Same as with Critical, except (presumably) less extreme values.
- **Occurrences** – The number of occurrences required to trip the threshold.

Control Automated Maintenance Tasks

Three Automated Tasks

Oracle has automated tasks that are executed at regular intervals to perform maintenance operations on the system. Automated maintenance tasks are run during predefined maintenance windows on your database. Maintenance windows are predefined time intervals that are intended to occur during a period of low system load. Maintenance windows can be customized to fit the resource usage patterns of your database. You can also disable some or all of the default windows from running or create your own maintenance windows.

Oracle 11G has three predefined automated maintenance tasks that are configured to run in all maintenance windows by default:

- **Automatic Optimizer Statistics Collection** - This task collects optimizer statistics for all schema objects in the database for which there are no statistics or only stale statistics. The statistics are used by the SQL query optimizer to improve the performance of SQL execution.
- **Automatic Segment Advisor** - This task identifies segments that have space available for reclamation, and makes recommendations on how to defragment those segments.
- **Automatic SQL Tuning Advisor** - This task is new with Oracle 11G. It examines the performance of high-load SQL statements, and makes recommendations, along with a rationale for each recommendation and its expected benefit. The recommendation relates to: collection of statistics on objects; creation of new indexes; restructuring of the SQL statement; or creation of a SQL Profile. The only recommendation that the Automatic SQL Tuning Advisor can implement automatically is adding a SQL profile.

Predefined Maintenance Windows

Oracle 11G has seven predefined maintenance windows, one for each day of the week. The weekday windows run four hours – 10:00pm to 2:00am. The weekend windows run 20 hours, 6:00am through 2:00AM the following day. As mentioned earlier, you can change or disable any of the predefined windows or add one or more of your own. During long maintenance windows, all automated maintenance tasks except Automatic SQL Tuning Advisor are restarted every four hours. This ensures that maintenance tasks are run regularly, regardless of window size.

```
MONDAY_WINDOW     10P Monday    -> 2AM Tuesday
TUESDAY_WINDOW    10P Tuesday   -> 2AM Wednesday
WEDNESAY_WINDOW   10P Wednesday -> 2AM Thursday
THURSDAY_WINDOW   10P Thursday  -> 2AM Friday
FRIDAY_WINDOW     10P Friday    -> 2AM Saturday
SATURDAY_WINDOW   6A Saturday   -> 2AM Sunday
SUNDAY_WINDOW     6A Sunday     -> 2AM Monday
```

Autotask Background Process (ABP)

In Oracle Database 11g, the new Auto-Task background process can run hundreds or thousands of jobs in the manageability windows. It interfaces with the Oracle scheduler to manage the job load imposed by the automated maintenance tasks. ABP provides out-of-the-box management of resource distribution (CPU and I/O) among the various database maintenance tasks. CPU load is automatically managed. I/O is managed only if the I/O Resource Manager is enabled. ABP ensures that the operation of the database during maintenance operations is not adversely affected and that user activity gets the necessary resources to complete.

The ABP process is started at the beginning of each maintenance window by MMON. Once started, it converts tasks into scheduler jobs for execution. The jobs are assigned using three priority levels: urgent, high, and medium. The ABP uses these priority levels when assigning tasks to consumer groups in the DEFAULT_MAINTENANCE_PLAN. ABP maintains

History in the SYSAUX tablespace of all automated maintenance task executions. You can view this repository using the DBA_AUTOTASK_TASK view.

Disabling a Maintenance Task

By default, all maintenance tasks run in all predefined maintenance windows. It's possible to disable a maintenance task for a specific window using the DBMS_AUTO_TASK_ADMIN.DISABLE procedure. The following example disables the Automatic SQL Tuning Advisor from running in the window FRIDAY_WINDOW:

```
BEGIN
  DBMS_AUTO_TASK_ADMIN.DISABLE(
  client_name => 'sql tuning advisor',
  operation => NULL,
  window_name => 'FRIDAY_WINDOW');
END;
```

To disable the job in all windows, you would pass a NULL to the window_name parameter:

```
BEGIN
  DBMS_AUTO_TASK_ADMIN.DISABLE(
  client_name => 'sql tuning advisor',
  operation => NULL,
  window_name => NULL);
END;
```

Enabling a Maintenance Task

To enable this maintenance task in a single window, use the ENABLE procedure, as follows:

```
BEGIN
  dbms_auto_task_admin.enable(
  client_name => 'sql tuning advisor',
  operation => NULL,
  window_name => 'FRIDAY');
END;
```

And to enable the SQL Tuning Advisor in all windows, pass a NULL to the window_name parameter:
```
BEGIN
  dbms_auto_task_admin.enable(
  client_name => 'sql tuning advisor',
  operation => NULL,
  window_name => NULL);
END;
```

Database Resource Manager New Features
Database Resource Manager

The Oracle Database Resource Manager (DRM) is designed to optimize resource allocation among concurrent database sessions. It attempts to prevent problems that can happen if the operating system makes resource decisions when presented with high overhead without having awareness of the database needs. DRM helps to overcome these problems by giving the database more control over how hardware resources are allocated. DRM enables you to classify sessions into groups based on session attributes, and then allocate resources to those groups in a way that optimizes hardware utilization for your application environment. The information that performs the functions of classifying sessions and assigning resources is called a resource plan. Oracle 11G comes with sophisticated new built-in resource plans for DRM. There is a mixed-workload plan that provides resource management for a mixed environment consisting of both OLTP and DSS/batch jobs. There is a Data Warehouse plan that provides resource management for a data warehousing environment. Finally there is the maintenance plan that provides resource management for the maintenance window. These plans are shipped with Oracle 11G and provide resource management directives that should provide immediate benefits for the majority of database installations. There are three elements of DRM:

- **Resource consumer group**: A group of sessions that are grouped together based on resource requirements.
- **Resource plan**: A container for directives that specify how resources are allocated to resource consumer groups.

- **Resource plan directive**: Associates a resource consumer group with a particular plan and specifies how resources are to be allocated to that resource consumer group.

Resource Plan Directives

A resource plan directive for a consumer group, can specify limits for CPU and I/O resource consumption for sessions in that group. This is done by specifying the action to be taken if a call within a session exceeds one of the specified limits. These actions, called switches, occur only for sessions that are running and consuming resources, not waiting for user input or for CPU cycles. The possible actions are the following:

- The session is switched to a consumer group with lower resource allocations.
- The session is killed (terminated).
- The session's current SQL statement is aborted.

The resource plan directive attribute that determines which of the above three actions will be taken is SWITCH_GROUP. This attribute specifies the consumer group to which a session is switched if the specified criteria are met. If the value of this parameter is a consumer group, the session will be switched to that group. If the group name is 'CANCEL_SQL', the current call for that session is canceled. Finally, if the group name is 'KILL_SESSION', then the session is killed.

Per session I/O or CPU Limits

The resource plan directive attributes that can be used in specifying the criteria to use in making switch determinations follow. If not set, all default to UNLIMITED.

- **SWITCH_TIME**: Specifies the time (in CPU seconds) that a call can execute before an action is taken.
- **SWITCH_IO_MEGABYTES**: Specifies the number of megabytes of I/O that a session can transfer (read and write) before being switched.
- **SWITCH_IO_REQS**: Specifies the number of I/O requests that a session can execute before an action is taken.

Be sure you understand the meaning of and difference between the two criteria for the test.

SWITCH_ESTIMATE and SWITCH_FOR_CALL

These two resource plan attributes can be used to modify the behavior of resource plan switching:

- **SWITCH_ESTIMATE**: If TRUE, the database estimates the execution time of each call. If the estimated execution time exceeds SWITCH_TIME, the session is moved to the SWITCH_GROUP before beginning the call. The default is FALSE.
- **SWITCH_FOR_CALL**: If TRUE, a session that was automatically switched to another consumer group is returned to its original consumer group when the top level call completes. The default is NULL.

Using new scheduler features

Lightweight Jobs

New with Oracle 11G is the concept of lightweight jobs. In comparison with traditional DBMS_SCHEDULER jobs, lightweight jobs have lower creation overhead and generate less redo. You'd use lightweight jobs when you have a large number of short-duration jobs that run frequently. Lightweight jobs have the following characteristics:

- Unlike regular jobs, they are not schema objects.
- They have a significant improvement in create and drop time over regular jobs because they do not have the overhead of creating a schema object.
- They have lower average session creation time than regular jobs.
- They have a small footprint on disk for job metadata and runtime data.

Lightweight jobs can only be generated via a job template. You create a lightweight job by using the job_style attribute 'LIGHTWEIGHT' while creating the template. The alternative job_style is 'REGULAR', which is the default. Like programs and schedules, regular jobs are schema objects. A regular job offers more flexibility but entails more overhead when it is created or dropped. A lightweight job must reference a program object to specify a job action. The program must be enabled when the lightweight job is created, and the program type must be either 'PLSQL_BLOCK' or 'STORED_PROCEDURE'. You cannot grant privileges on lightweight jobs. They inherit privileges from the specified program. A user with privileges on the program being called has corresponding privileges on the lightweight job.

Job Arrays

If you have a need to create many jobs at once, you might be able to reduce transaction overhead if you use the CREATE_JOBS procedure. It's possible to use this procedure to create multiple jobs in a single transaction using the new SYS.JOBARRAY type. The actual process to create a job array is extremely unlikely to appear on the test, but you might see a question about the new capability.

Remote External Jobs

New in 11g, the Oracle Scheduler can schedule and run external jobs on a remote host. The remote host does not need to have an Oracle database, but it must have a Scheduler agent installed it. This will allow the scheduling database to start jobs on that host and receive job output and error information. The agent must be registered with every database that will be starting remote jobs on it. In addition, before a database can run external jobs, an initial setup is required. This setup enables secure communications between the database and remote Scheduler agents.

The steps to set up the database to run remote external jobs are:

1. Using SQL*Plus, connect to the database as the SYS user.
2. Enter the following command to verify that the XML DB option is installed: **SQL> DESC RESOURCE_VIEW**. If XML DB is not installed, this command returns an "object does not exist" error.
3. Enable HTTP connections to the database by submitting the following command: **exec DBMS_XDB.SETHTTPPORT(port);** where **port** is the TCP port number on which you want the database to listen for HTTP connections.
4. Run the script prvtrsch.plb with following command: **SQL> @?/rdbms/admin/prvtrsch.plb**
5. Set a registration password for the Scheduler agents using the **SET_AGENT_REGISTRATION_PASS** procedure.

To install and configure the Scheduler Agent:

1. Use the Oracle Installer to install the product option Oracle Scheduler Agent.
2. Use a text editor to review the agent configuration parameter file **schagent.conf**, which is located in the Scheduler agent home directory, and verify the port number in the PORT= directive. You will need this port number when creating remote external jobs.
3. Ensure that any firewall software on the remote host or any other firewall that protects that host has an exception to accommodate the Scheduler agent.

4. Register the Scheduler agent with a database that is to run remote external jobs on the agent's host computer. Use the following command: **AGENT_HOME/bin/schagent -registerdatabase db_host db_http_port**; where: db_host is the host name or IP address of the host on which the database resides, and db_http_port is the port number that the database listens on for HTTP connections.
5. The agent prompts you to enter the agent registration password that you set in
6. (UNIX and Linux only) Start the Scheduler agent with the following command: **AGENT_HOME/bin/schagent -start**

Performance Enhancements

ADDM Enhancements

Real Application Clusters

ADDM has been enhanced to provide performance diagnostic and tuning advice for all nodes in a Real Application Cluster. A new mode of ADDM analyzes an Oracle RAC database and reports issues that affect the entire cluster in addition to those that are affecting individual instances. The new capability is of particular use for global resources such as interconnect traffic and I/O. It simplifies the task of tuning RAC databases and makes the results more precise. When using ADDM in a RAC database, you have the option of running it in any of three modes:

- **Database** -- Provides metrics for the entire cluster.
- **Instance** -- Provides metrics for a single instance.
- **Partial** -- Provides metrics for more than one, but not all nodes in the cluster.

DBMS_ADDM Package

Oracle suggests using Oracle Enterprise Manager as the primary interface for diagnostic monitoring. However, it's also possible to run ADDM using the DBMS_ADDM package. In order to run the DBMS_ADDM APIs, the user must be granted the ADVISOR privilege.

- **DBMS_ADDM.ANALYZE_DB** - Run ADDM in Database Mode.
- **DBMS_ADDM.ANALYZE_INST** - Run ADDM in Instance Mode.
- **DBMS_ADDM.ANALYZE_PARTIAL** - Run ADDM in Partial Mode.
- **SELECT DBMS_ADDM.GET_REPORT(:task_name) FROM DUAL;** - Display an ADDM Report.

Findings and Directives

ADDM analysis results are represented as a set of findings. Findings come in four classes:

- **Problem** findings describe the root cause of a database performance problem.
- **Symptom** findings contain information that often leads to one or more problem findings.
- **Information** findings report information that provides background data, but does not constitute a performance problem.
- **Warning** findings contain information about problems that may affect the accuracy of the ADDM analysis.

Directives alter the recommendations provided by ADDM, by filtering the result set or eliminating certain finding types altogether. The DBMS_ADDM package has several INSERT…DIRECTIVE procedures:

- **INSERT_FINDING_DIRECTIVE** - Limit reporting of a specific finding type.
- **INSERT_PARAMETER_DIRECTIVE** - Prevents ADDM from creating actions to alter the value of a specific system parameter
- **INSERT_SEGMENT_DIRECTIVE** - Prevents ADDM from creating actions to "run Segment Advisor" for specific segments
- **INSERT_SQL_DIRECTIVE** - Creates a directive to limit reporting of actions on specific SQL

Each of the INSERT…DIRECTIVE procedures has a corresponding DELETE…DIRECTIVE procedure that removes a directive thus created.

New Views

You can locate ADDM information through the DBA_ADVISOR views:

- **DBA_ADVISOR_FINDINGS** - Displays all the findings discovered by all advisors.

- **DBA_ADVISOR_FINDING_NAMES** - List of all finding names registered with the advisor framework.
- **DBA_ADVISOR_RECOMMENDATIONS** - Displays the results of completed diagnostic tasks with recommendations for the problems identified in each execution.
- **DBA_ADVISOR_TASKS** - Provides basic information about existing tasks, such as the task ID, task name, and when the task was created.

Setup Automatic Memory Management

In Oracle 10G, the then-new parameters **sga_target** and **pga_target** automated much of the previously complex task of tuning the SGA and PGA memory areas in a database. Prior to 10G, there were half a dozen parameters to tweak various pools of memory. In Oracle 11G, memory management has gone a step further. The new **memory_target** parameter is the only value that needs to be set to allow Oracle to automatically manage memory. You need to understand what it does, and how these four parameters relate to each other when set (or not set).

memory_target

When MEMORY_TARGET is set, the database will allocate this much memory on startup, by default granting 60% to the SGA and 40% to the PGA. Over time, as the database runs, it will redistribute memory as needed between the system global area (SGA) and the instance program global area (instance PGA). If MEMORY_TARGET is not set, automatic memory management is not enabled, even if you have set a value for MEMORY_MAX_TARGET.

memory_max_target

When set, this determines the maximum amount of memory that Oracle will grab from the OS for the SGA and PGA. If this value is not set, it will default to the MEMORY_TARGET value.

sga_target

This value is not required in 11G if using automatic memory management. If this value is set and MEMORY_TARGET is also set, then the value of SGA_TARGET becomes the <u>minimum</u> amount of memory allocated to the SGA by automatic memory management.

pga_aggregate_target

This value is not required in 11G if using automatic memory management. If this value is set and MEMORY_TARGET is also set, then the value of PGA_AGGREGATE_TARGET becomes the <u>minimum</u> amount of memory allocated to the PGA by automatic memory management.

Enhancements in statistics collection

Pending Statistics

Starting with the 11g Release, it's possible to automatically publish the statistics at the end of the gather operation (the default behavior), or to have the new statistics saved as pending. When saved as pending, you can validate the new statistics and publish them only if they generate acceptable optimizer plans. The following command will return 'TRUE' if statistics will be published when they are gathered, or FALSE if the statistics will be kept pending.

```
SELECT DBMS_STATS.GET_PREFS('PUBLISH') publish
FROM   dual;
```

You can change the PUBLISH setting at either the schema or the table level. By default, the optimizer uses only published statistics in generating plans. If you want the optimizer to use pending statistics, you may set the initialization parameter
OPTIMIZER_USE_PENDING_STATISTICS to TRUE (the default value is FALSE). You may publish pending stats for a single table, single schema, or the entire database with the DBMS_STATS.PUBLISH_PENDING_STATS procedure;

- Database - **DBMS_STATS.PUBLISH_PENDING_STATS (NULL, NULL);**
- Schema - **DBMS_STATS.PUBLISH_PENDING_STATS (schema_name, NULL);**
- Table - **DBMS_STATS.PUBLISH_PENDING_STATS (schema_name, table_name);**

GRANULARITY AND INCREMENTAL parameters

For partitioned tables and indexes, DBMS_STATS can gather separate statistics for each partition and global statistics for the entire table or index. The type of partitioning statistics to be gathered is specified in the GRANULARITY argument of the DBMS_STATS gathering procedures. Both types can be important for creating good plans. Oracle recommends setting the GRANULARITY parameter to AUTO to gather both types of partition statistics.

With partitioned tables, new data is often loaded into a new partition. As new partitions are added and data loaded, statistics must be gathered on the new partition, and global statistics must be kept up to date for the entire table. If the INCREMENTAL value for a partition table is set to TRUE, and you gather statistics on that table with the GRANULARITY parameter set to AUTO, Oracle will gather statistics on the new partition and update the global table statistics by scanning only those partitions that have been modified rather than the entire table. If the INCREMENTAL value for the partitioned table is set to FALSE (the default value), then a full table scan is used to maintain the global statistics. This is a highly resource intensive and time consuming operation for large tables. Setting INCREMENTAL to TRUE for a partitioned table requires the SYSAUX tablespace to consume additional space to maintain the global statistics.

New sampling technique

Gathering statistics for a large table can be very time-consuming if the operation reads every row. Sampling a small percentage of the rows provides a much faster operation, albeit with less reliable metrics. The sample size is specified using the ESTIMATE_PERCENT argument of the DBMS_STATS procedures. Prior to 11G, this value has been set to a static value, commonly 5, 10, or 15%. With 11G, Oracle recommends setting the parameter to the new function DBMS_STATS.AUTO_SAMPLE_SIZE. This new function is designed to maximize performance gains while achieving necessary statistical accuracy. AUTO_SAMPLE_SIZE lets Oracle determine the best sample size necessary for good statistics, based on the statistical properties of the particular object.

Multi-Column Statistics

When multiple columns from a single table are used together in the where clause of a query, the relationship between the columns can strongly affect the combined selectivity for the column group. For example, consider a table that has city and state columns. Selecting city and state together produces a much smaller cardinality result than selecting state alone. In 11G, it is possible to create extended statistics against two or more columns. The resulting metrics can be used by the optimizer to provide better access plans when both columns appear in a query.

```
BEGIN
  cg_name := dbms_stats.create_extended_stats
             (null,'customer_data',
             '(cust_state,cust_city)');
END;
/


SELECT sys.dbms_stats.show_extended_stats_name
         ('sh','customer_data',
         '(cust_state,cust_city)') col_group_name
FROM dual;
```

You will obtain an output similar to the following:

```
COL_GROUP_NAME
----------------
SYS_STU#S#WF25Z#QAHIHE#MOFFMM
```

Expression Statistics

When a function is applied to a column in the where clause of a query (function(col1)=constant), the optimizer has no way of knowing how that function will affect the selectivity of the column. By gathering expression statistics on the expression function(col1), the optimizer will have a more accurate selectivity value. You can also use the **create_extended_stats** function to accomplish this:

```
SELECT dbms_stats.create_extended_stats
                (null,'customer_data',
                '(lower(cust_city))')
FROM    dual;
```

Partitioning and Storage Enhancements

Implement the new partitioning methods

Interval Partitioning

Range partitioning maps data to partitions using ranges of key values that you establish for each partition. Interval partitioning is an extension of this concept. With interval partitioning, you instruct the database to automatically create partitions of a specified interval when inserted data exceeds the range partitions. The table must have at least one range partition. The range partitioning key value determines the high value of the range partitions -- called the transition point. The database will create interval partitions for data beyond that point.

Interval partitioning has the following restrictions:

- You can only specify one partitioning key column, and it must be of NUMBER or DATE type.
- Interval partitioning is not supported for index-organized tables.
- You cannot create a domain index on an interval-partitioned table.

Reference Partitioning

Reference partitioning is used with two tables that are related to one another by referential constraints. The partitioning key is inherited through an existing parent-child relationship, and it is enforced by enabled and active primary key and foreign key constraints. With this partitioning method, dependent tables with a child relationship can be logically equi-partitioned by inheriting the partitioning key from the parent table. The reference dependency will automatically cascade partition maintenance operations. For example, take a parent table of Orders, with a child table of order items with an enforced foreign key relationship. If Orders were to be partitioned by year, using the "Order

Date" column, the OrderItems table could be reference partitioned and would be partitioned by the 'Order Date' column even though that column is not part of the OrderItems table.

System Partitioning

System partitioning is different from every other partitioning method in that there is no partition key. System partitioning is application-controlled partitioning where the Oracle database is not controlling the data placement. The database allows the application to break a table into partitions without knowing what the individual partitions are for. All partitioning functions are controlled entirely by the application. Inserting a row into a system partitioned table without explicitly specifying a partition will fail. System partitioning does not provide performance enhancements as partition pruning and partition-wise joins are not possible with it.

Partitioning on Virtual Columns

Prior to 11G, a table could only be partitioned if the partitioning key physically existed in the table. In 11G it's possible for a partitioning key to be defined by an expression using one or more existing columns of a table. Virtual column-based Partitioning is supported with all basic partitioning strategies, including interval and composite partitioning.

Additional Composite Partitioning

Composite partitioning is a combination of two partitioning operations. A table is partitioned by one data distribution method and then each partition is further subdivided into subpartitions using a second logic. The subpartitions for a given partition represent a logical subset of the data. The two operations might be the same partition style (i.e. both Range), or different styles. The valid combinations of composite partitioning in 11G are:

- Range-Range; Range-Hash; Range-List
- List-Range; List-Hash; List-List
- Interval-Range; Interval-Hash; Interval-List

Employ Data Compression

Enhanced Table Compression

Table compression saves disk space and reduces memory use in the buffer cache. It can also speed up query execution during reads at the expense of incurring additional CPU overhead. Table compression is specified using the COMPRESS clause of the CREATE TABLE and ALTER TABLE statements. If compression is added to a table via ALTER TABLE, only data inserted or updated after the ALTER operation will be compressed. You can disable table compression with ALTER TABLE...NOCOMPRESS. In this case, all data that was already compressed remains compressed, and new data is inserted uncompressed. Table compression is transparent to applications.

You can enable compression for all table operations or you can enable it for direct-path inserts only. COMPATIBLE must be set to 11.1 or higher in order to enable compression for conventional DML. To enable compression for all operations you must use the COMPRESS FOR ALL OPERATIONS clause. To enable compression for direct-path inserts only, you use the COMPRESS FOR DIRECT_LOAD OPERATIONS clause. The keyword COMPRESS by itself is equivalent to the clause COMPRESS FOR DIRECT_LOAD OPERATIONS that existed in Oracle 10G.

New RMAN Compression: ZLIB

Prior to 11g Oracle RMAN used a single compression algorithm, called BZIP2. The algorithm performed very well in terms of the compression ratio in decreasing the size of RMAN files. However, it has a high CPU cost which makes it unsuitable for sites having CPU bottlenecks. With 11g, Oracle introduced a new compression algorithm, ZLIB. ZLIB is 40-50% faster than BZIP2 and has a compression ratio of about 1.68:1 to BZIP's 2:1. ZLIB is the default compression algorithm for RMAN in 11G. You can change this using the command:

```
RMAN> configure compression algorithm 'bzip2';
```

SecureFiles Compression

SecureFiles will be discussed further in a later chapter. However, I wanted to make a note here of the fact that this new data type has a built in capability for compression that is separate from the two already discussed.

SQL Access Advisor Overview

Optimizing access to data

Whereas SQL Tuning Advisor is designed to make sure that SQL statements are taking the most efficient path to provide the data requested, SQL Access Advisor is designed to help make sure that an efficient path to the data exists. SQL Access advisor offers recommendations intended to achieve the proper set of materialized views, materialized view logs, and indexes for a given workload. As a general rule, as the number of materialized views and indexes increase, query performance improves. SQL Access Advisor weighs trade-offs between space usage and query performance. SQL Access Advisor makes recommendations, each of which will contain one or more actions. If a recommendation contains multiple actions, all of the individual actions must be implemented to achieve the full benefit. If the Advisor decides that one or more base tables should be partitioned, it will collect all individual partition actions into a single recommendation. In that case, note that some or all of the remaining recommendations might be dependent on implementing the partitioning recommendation. It's not possible to view index and materialized view advice in isolation of the underlying table's partitioning.

Modes of Operation

SQL Access Advisor has two modes of operation: problem solving and evaluation. The default mode is problem solving. In this mode, SQL Access Advisor will attempt to solve access method problems by looking for new objects to create. When operating in evaluation mode, SQL Access Advisor will only comment on existing access paths that the given workload will use. A problem solving run might recommend creating a new index whereas an evaluation only scenario will only produce recommendations such as retaining an existing index. The evaluation mode is useful in determining which indexes and materialized views are actually being used by a given workload.

Intermediate Results

With 11G, SQL Access Advisor allows you to see intermediate results during the analysis operation. Previously, results were unavailable until the processing had completed or was interrupted by the user. With the change, it is possible to access results in the recommendation and action tables while the SQL Access Advisor task is still executing. Intermediate results represent recommendations only for the portion of the workload that has been executed up to that point in time. If the entire workload must be evaluated, then you should allow the task to complete normally. Recommendations made by the advisor early in the evaluation process will not have any base table partitioning recommendations. Partitioning analysis requires most of the workload to be processed before it's clear whether partitioning would be beneficial.

SQL Access Advisor using PL/SQL

Creating Tasks

You create advisor tasks to define what it is you want to analyze and where the analysis results should be placed. It's possible to create any number of tasks, each with a given specialization. All are based on the same Advisor task model and share the same repository. Tasks are created using the CREATE_TASK procedure:

```
VARIABLE task_id NUMBER;
VARIABLE task_name VARCHAR2(255);
EXECUTE :task_name := 'MYTASK';
EXECUTE DBMS_ADVISOR.CREATE_TASK
        ('SQL Access Advisor', :task_id, :task_name);
```

SQL Tuning Sets

The input workload for the SQL Access Advisor is the SQL Tuning Set. An important benefit of using a SQL Tuning Set is that because SQL Tuning Sets are stored as separate entities, they can be referenced by many Advisor tasks. A workload reference will be removed when a parent Advisor task is deleted or when the workload reference is removed from the Advisor task by the user. A SQL Tuning Set workload is created using DBMS_SQLTUNE. You can pull SQL Workload objects into a SQL Tuning Set using DBMS_ADVISOR:

```
EXECUTE
DBMS_ADVISOR.COPY_SQLWKLD_TO_STS('MYWORKLOAD','MYSTS','NEW');
```

Linking Tasks and Workloads

Tasks must be linked to a SQL Tuning Set in order to generate advisor recommendations. You create links with the ADD_STS_REF procedure, using their respective names to link the task to a Tuning Set. Once a connection has been defined, the SQL Tuning Set is protected from removal or update.

```
EXECUTE DBMS_ADVISOR.ADD_STS_REF('MYTASK', null,
'MYWORKLOAD');
```

Removing a Link

Before a task or a SQL Tuning Set workload can be deleted, any existing links between the task and the workload must be removed. Links are removed using the DELETE_STS_REF procedure.

```
EXECUTE DBMS_ADVISOR.DELETE_STS_REF('MYTASK', null,
'MYWORKLOAD');
```

Recommendation Options

Parameters for a given task must be defined using the SET_TASK_PARAMETER procedure before recommendations can be generated. If parameters are not defined, then the defaults are used. You can set task parameters by using the SET_TASK_PARAMETER procedure.

```
DBMS_ADVISOR.SET_TASK_PARAMETER (
     task_name IN VARCHAR2,
     parameter IN VARCHAR2,
     value IN [VARCHAR2 | NUMBER]);
```

Generating Recommendations

You can generate recommendations by using the EXECUTE_TASK procedure. After it completes, the DBA_ADVISOR_LOG table will show execution status and the number of recommendations and actions produced. EXECUTE_TASK is a synchronous operation, so control will not be returned to the user until the operation has completed, or is interrupted. Upon completion, you can check the DBA_ADVISOR_LOG table for the execution status. The recommendations can be queried by task name in DBA_ADVISOR_RECOMMENDATIONS and the actions in DBA_ADVISOR_ACTIONS.

```
EXECUTE DBMS_ADVISOR.EXECUTE_TASK('MYTASK');
```

Using RMAN Enhancements

Managing Archive logs

Oracle 11G simplifies archive log management when used by multiple components. The archivelog deletion policy can be used to ensure the logs are deleted only when they are no longer needed by required components (e.g. Data Guard, Streams, and Flashback). In a Data Guard environment, all standby destinations can be considered where logs are applied, before marking archive logs to be deleted. This configuration is specified using CONFIGURE ARCHIVELOG DELETION POLICY TO APPLIED ON ALL STANDBY.

In addition 11G increases availability when backing up archive logs. It allows an optional archive log destination to be utilized in the event that the flash recovery area is inaccessible during backup. If this happens, the backup will use a copy from the optional destination and continue backing up the archive logs.

Duplicating a Database

Requirements for active database duplication

The DUPLICATE command has been enhanced to allow cloning a database to a remote site directly over the network without requiring an existing backup. An ASM-to-ASM DUPLICATE over the network is also supported. There is no need to copy or move backups to the remote site before executing the DUPLICATE command. Some of the requirements for performing a DUPLICATE operation are:

- The Source database must be in MOUNT or OPEN status
- The Source and Destination databases must be on the same OS
- The Source and Destination databases must have password files with matched SYS passwords.

- The Source and Destination databases must be accessible via Oracle Net.

Filename Conversion

When duplicating a database, RMAN must generate names for the new database files. If you are performing a backup to a different host and the directory structure is exactly the same as the source host, then the exact same filenames can be used. In this case, you would specify the NOFILENAMECHECK option for the DUPLICATE command. If the directory structure is different, or if you want to name files differently, then you must specify patterns for DUPLICATE to use in renaming the files. You can rename the control files, data files, online redo log files, and tempfiles. There are DUPLICATE parameters to handle each of these.

- **db_file_name_convert** -- Allows you to set a pattern for renaming datafiles
  db_file_name_convert '/u02/app/oracle','u04/app/oracle'
- **spfile...log_file_name_convert** -- Allows you to set a pattern for renaming log files
  spfile...set log_file_name_convert '/u02/app/oracle','u04/app/oracle'
- **spfile...parameter_value_convert** -- Allows you to set a pattern conversion for all parameters with directory paths <u>except</u> database files and log files.
  spfile...parameter_value_convert '/u02/app/oracle','u04/app/oracle'

```
RMAN> duplicate database to database2
2> from active database
3> db_file_name_convert '/u02/app/oracle','u04/app/oracle'
4> spfile
5> set log_file_name_convert '/u02/app/oracle',
'u04/app/oracle'
6> parameter_value_convert '/u02/app/oracle',
'u04/app/oracle';
```

Back up large files in sections

Multisection backups

New with RMAN in 11G is the SECTION SIZE parameter. If this parameter is set, RMAN can create a multisection backup. When performing a multisection backup, RMAN creates a backup piece of the value specified that contains one contiguous range of blocks from the file being backed up. Each piece of a multisection backup is the same size, with the exception of the final piece, which will be whatever is left over. By backing a file up in sections, RMAN can process each of the sections independently and in parallel using multiple channels. When a SECTION SIZE value is specified that is larger than the file being backed up, RMAN will not make use of multisection backup. If a section size is specified that will result in more than 256 sections, RMAN will increase the section size to a value that results in exactly 256 sections.

Perform Archival Backups

All-inclusive backup

The RMAN KEEP option specifies that a backup be created as an archival backup. An archival backup is a self-contained backup that is exempt from the configured retention policy. Archival backups contain all of the files necessary to restore the backup and recover it to a consistent state. If the database is open at the time an archival backup is created, RMAN automatically generates and backs up the redo logs needed to make the backup consistent. When available, RMAN will use archival backups for disaster recovery restore operations. However, their intended purpose is to produce a snapshot of the database that can be restored on another system for testing or historical usage.

KEEP

When computing the retention policy RMAN does not consider backup pieces with the KEEP option. The KEEP option cannot be used to override the retention policy for files stored in the flash recovery area. When KEEP is specified, RMAN backs up datafiles, archived redo logs, the control file, and the server parameter file. A recovery catalog is required when KEEP FOREVER is specified because the backup records will eventually age out of the control file.

UNTIL TIME 'date_string'

This clause specifies an end date for retaining the RMAN backup or copy. After this date the backup is obsolete, regardless of the backup retention policy settings. It's possible to provide a specific date/time by using the current NLS_DATE_FORMAT, or a SQL date expression such as 'SYSDATE+90'. If a KEEP TIME is provided with a date only, then the backup becomes obsolete one second after midnight on that date.

RESTORE POINT restore_point_name

Creates a restore point matching the SCN to which RMAN must recover the backup to a consistent state. The name provided must not already exist. RMAN captures the SCN immediately after the datafile backups complete. The restore point acts as a label for the SCN to which this archival backup can be restored.

NOKEEP

This option indicates that any KEEP attributes no longer apply to the backup. After specifying NOKEEP, the backup is subject to the configured backup retention

Manage Recovery Catalogs

Merging Recovery Catalogs

In 11G, RMAN has a new command, IMPORT CATALOG, which allows you to import the metadata from one recovery catalog schema into a different catalog schema. If you currently have catalog schemas residing on multiple databases, this command enables you to merge them all to a single catalog schema. To import a catalog, RMAN must be connected to the catalog into which you want to import the catalog data. The destination cannot be a virtual private catalog. The version of the source recovery catalog schema must be equal to the current version of the RMAN executable. The same database cannot be registered in both the source and destination catalog schemas. If this is the case, then UNREGISTER this database from the source recovery catalog and execute the IMPORT command again. By default, the imported database IDs are unregistered from the source recovery catalog schema after being imported. If there are name conflicts with global scripts during import because the destination schema already contains the script name, RMAN renames the global script name to "COPY OF script_name".

Create a Virtual Private Catalog

In 11G RMAN introduces the concept of a virtual private catalog. A virtual private catalog is a set of synonyms and views that enable user access to a subset of the base recovery catalog. Prior to 11G access to the RMAN recovery catalog was an all-or-nothing proposition. Now it's possible to grant catalog access for a specific subset of databases to a given user. The owner of the base recovery catalog can GRANT or REVOKE restricted access to the catalog. Each VPC user has full read/write access to the metadata in the virtual private catalog granted to them. The RMAN metadata is stored in the schema of the virtual private catalog owner. Virtual catalog users cannot modify global RMAN scripts, although they can execute them.

Steps in creating a Virtual Private Catalog

Creating a virtual private catalog for a database user involves four steps from three locations. The first two steps are from the SQL*Plus as a user with admin privileges. The third step is executed from RMAN as the base catalog owner. The fourth step is executed from RMAN as the virtual private catalog user. The four steps are:

1. Create the VPC User.
2. Grant recovery_catalog_owner to the VPC user.
3. Grant the catalog to the new VPC user.
4. Create the virtual catalog.

From SQL*Plus, connected to the base recovery catalog database with administrator privileges:

```
SQL> CREATE USER vpc1 IDENTIFIED BY password
2 DEFAULT TABLESPACE vpcusers
3 QUOTA UNLIMITED ON vpcusers;
SQL> GRANT recovery_catalog_owner TO vpc1;
SQL> EXIT
```

From RMAN, connected to the recovery catalog database as the catalog owner catowner:

```
RMAN> CONNECT CATALOG catowner@catdb
recovery catalog database Password: password
connected to recovery catalog database
RMAN> GRANT CATALOG FOR DATABASE prod1 TO vpc1;
RMAN> EXIT;
```

From RMAN connected to the recovery catalog database as the virtual private catalog owner:

```
RMAN> CONNECT CATALOG vpc1@catdb
recovery catalog database Password: password
connected to recovery catalog database
RMAN> CREATE VIRTUAL CATALOG;
RMAN> EXIT;
```

Using Flashback and Logminer

Overview of Flashback Data Archive

What is Flashback Data Archive

Oracle 11G's new Flashback Data Archive feature allows you to store table-level change history for extended periods of time. It provides the ability to track all transactional changes to a table over its lifetime. The Flashback Data Archive functionality is useful to maintain compliance with record storage policies and audit reports. It's possible to have multiple Flashback Data Archives in a single database, one of which can be (although it's not required), specified as the default for the database. Each Flashback Data Archive in a database is configured with a retention time that determines how long data stored in that particular archive is to be retained.

Flashback archiving is off for any table by default. You can enable flashback archiving for a table if all of the following are true:

- You have the FLASHBACK ARCHIVE object privilege on the Flashback Data Archive that you want to use for that table.
- The table you want to archive is not nested, clustered, temporary, remote, or external.
- The table does not contain LONG or nested columns.

Once flashback archiving is enabled for a table, you can disable it only if you either have the FLASHBACK ARCHIVE ADMINISTER system privilege or you are logged into the database with SYSDBA privileges. While flashback archiving is enabled for a table, some DDL statements are not allowed on it and will generate an ORA-55610 error. Unfortunately from a testing standpoint, many of the disallowed statements under 11g Release 1 are allowed under Release 2. In 11GR1, the disallowed operations are:

- Dropping, renaming, or modifying a column via ALTER_TABLE
- Performing partition or subpartition operations
- Converting a LONG column to a LOB column

- An ALTER TABLE..UPGRADE TABLE operation
- DROP TABLE statement
- RENAME TABLE statement
- TRUNCATE TABLE statement

In 11G Release 2, only the following operations are disallowed:

- ALTER TABLE statement that includes an UPGRADE TABLE clause, with or without an INCLUDING DATA clause
- ALTER TABLE statement that moves or exchanges a partition or subpartition operation
- DROP TABLE statement

Benefits

Flashback Data Archive can be the solution to any number of business requirements. Many government agencies and organizations require that data be kept for a set number of years before being deleted. The settings of a Flashback Data Archive can be specifically configured to meet these requirements. After the specified time period has expired, the data will automatically be aged out of the archive – effectively 'shredding' it without requiring direct intervention. It can help in satisfying some of the storage requirements for such legislative acts as Sarbanes-Oxley and HIPAA. It can provide a source of data for audits. Flashback data archive can also be used as a simple method to recover accidentally altered or deleted data.

Manage Flashback Data Archive

Flashback Data Archive Creation and Maintenance

A Flashback Data Archive is created using the CREATE FLASHBACK ARCHIVE statement. If you are logged on with SYSDBA privileges, you can also specify that this is the default Flashback Data Archive for the system. When creating a new flashback data archive, you must specify the following:

- Name of the Flashback Data Archive
- Name of the first tablespace of the Flashback Data Archive
- Retention time (number of days that Flashback Data Archive data for the table is guaranteed to be stored)
- (Optional) Maximum amount of space that the Flashback Data Archive can use in the first tablespace. The default is unlimited.

Create a default Flashback Data Archive named fda1 using a maximum of 15 Gigs of tablespace fda_tbs1. The data will be retained for two years:

```
CREATE FLASHBACK ARCHIVE DEFAULT fda1
TABLESPACE fda_tbs1 QUOTA 15G RETENTION 2 YEAR;
```

Create a Flashback Data Archive named fda2 that uses tablespace fda_tbs2, whose data will be retained for three years:

```
CREATE FLASHBACK ARCHIVE fda2
TABLESPACE fda_tbs2 RETENTION 3 YEAR;
```

Using the ALTER FLASHBACK ARCHIVE statement, you can change the retention time of a Flashback Data Archive; purge some or all of its data; and add, modify, or remove tablespaces. If you are logged on with SYSDBA privileges, you can also make a specific archive the default Flashback Data Archive for the system.

- Make Flashback Data Archive fla1 the default Flashback Data Archive:
  ```
  ALTER FLASHBACK ARCHIVE fda1 SET DEFAULT;
  ```

- Add an additional 5Gigs quota of tablespace fda_tbs1 to Flashback Data Archive fda1:
  ```
  ALTER FLASHBACK ARCHIVE fda1
  ADD TABLESPACE da_tbs1 QUOTA 5G;
  ```

- Add unlimited quota on tablespace fda_tbs3 to Flashback Data Archive fda1:
  ```
  ALTER FLASHBACK ARCHIVE fda1 ADD TABLESPACE tbs3;
  ```

- Change the retention time for Flashback Data Archive fda1 to four years:

```
ALTER FLASHBACK ARCHIVE fda1 MODIFY RETENTION 4 YEAR;
```

- Purge all historical data older than one day from Flashback Data Archive fda1:
  ```
  ALTER FLASHBACK ARCHIVE fda1
  PURGE BEFORE TIMESTAMP (SYSTIMESTAMP - INTERVAL '1'
  DAY);
  ```

You can drop a Flashback Data Archive with the DROP FLASHBACK ARCHIVE statement. This statement will delete its historical data, but will not drop the tablespace the archive was stored on.

Remove Flashback Data Archive fda1 and all its historical data:
```
DROP FLASHBACK ARCHIVE fda1;
```

Setting Tables to use Flashback Archive

Flashback archiving is disabled for all tables by default. If a flashback data archive exists in the database, and you have the FLASHBACK ARCHIVE privilege on it, you can enable flashback archiving for a table. To enable flashback archiving for a table, you use the FLASHBACK ARCHIVE clause in either a CREATE TABLE or ALTER TABLE statement. It's possible to set the specific Flashback Data Archive where the data for the table will be stored in the FLASHBACK ARCHIVE clause. If no clause is provided, the default Flashback Data Archive for the database will be used. Some examples of making tables use flashback archiving follow:

- Create table dept and use the default Flashback Data Archive:
  ```
  CREATE TABLE dept (DEPTNO NUMBER(4) NOT NULL,
                    DEPTNAME VARCHAR2(10))
  FLASHBACK ARCHIVE;
  ```

- Create table dept and use the Flashback Data Archive fda1:
  ```
  CREATE TABLE dept (DEPTNO NUMBER(4) NOT NULL,
                    DEPTNAME VARCHAR2(10))
  FLASHBACK ARCHIVE fda1;
  ```

- Enable flashback archiving for the table dept and use the default Flashback Data Archive:
  ```
  ALTER TABLE dept FLASHBACK ARCHIVE;
  ```

- Enable flashback archiving for the table dept and use the Flashback Data Archive fda1:
  ```
  ALTER TABLE dept FLASHBACK ARCHIVE fda1;
  ```

- Disable flashback archiving for the table dept:
  ```
  ALTER TABLE dept NO FLASHBACK ARCHIVE;
  ```

Flashback Data Archive Views

The following new views in the data dictionary are specific to the Flashback Data Archive:

- DBA_FLASHBACK_ARCHIVE_TABLES
- DBA_FLASHBACK_ARCHIVE
- DBA_FLASHBACK_ARCHIVE_TS

Back-out transactions using Flashback

Flashback Transaction Backout

You can use the DBMS_FLASHBACK.TRANSACTION_BACKOUT procedure to roll back a transaction and its dependent transactions while the database remains online. Transaction backout uses undo data to create and execute the compensating transactions to return the affected data to its original state. TRANSACTION_BACKOUT does not commit the DML operations that it performs as part of transaction backout. However, it does hold all the required locks on rows and tables in the right form to prevent other dependencies from entering the system. To make the transaction backout permanent, you must explicitly commit the transaction.

In order to configure a database for the Oracle Flashback Transaction Query feature, the database must be running in ARCHIVELOG mode. In addition, the database administrator must enable supplemental logging.

```
ALTER DATABASE ADD SUPPLEMENTAL LOG DATA;
```

To perform Oracle Flashback Query operations, the administrator must grant appropriate privileges to the user who will be performing them. For Oracle Flashback Query, the administrator can do either of the following:

- To allow access to specific objects during queries, grant FLASHBACK and SELECT privileges on those objects.
- To allow queries on all tables, grant the FLASHBACK ANY TABLE privilege.

For Oracle Flashback Transaction Query, the administrator will need to grant the **SELECT ANY TRANSACTION** privilege. To allow execution of undo SQL code retrieved by an Oracle Flashback Transaction, the administrator will need to grant: **SELECT, UPDATE, DELETE, and INSERT privileges** for the appropriate tables. Finally, the administrator will need to grant the user **EXECUTE privileges on the DBMS_FLASHBACK** Package.

Dependent Transactions

When you are tolling back a given transaction, there may be one or more dependant transactions. A dependent transaction is related by either a **write-after-write (WAW)** relationship, in which a transaction modifies the same data that was changed by the target transaction, or a **Primary Key Constraint** relationship, in which a transaction re-inserts the same primary key value that was deleted by the target transaction.

Backout Options

There are four options to TRANSACTION_BACKOUT. You're almost certain to see a question referencing this information on the test. The four options determine how the backout operation will handle any transactions that are dependent on the one being backed out:

- **CASCADE** -- Backs out specified transactions and all dependent transactions in reverse-order (children are backed out before parents are backed out).
- **NOCASCADE** -- This is the default option. It assumes there are no dependent transactions. If a dependent transaction exists, it will cause an error.
- **NOCASCADE_FORCE** -- Backs out specified transactions. If there are any dependent transactions, they are ignored. The server executes undo SQL statements for specified transactions in the reverse order of commit times.
- **NONCONFLICT_ONLY** -- Backs out changes to non-conflicting rows of the specified transactions.

Working with Logminer

New Oracle Enterprise Manager Screen

In Oracle 11G, it is possible to use the Oracle Enterprise Manager Database Control interface for LogMiner. Prior to 11G, administrators were required to use the standalone Java Console to use LogMiner. The Java Console was not integrated with the rest of Enterprise Manager. With this new interface, administrators have a much more intuitive means for using LogMiner. The task-based work flows enable log mining and are integrated with Flashback Transactions.

Diagnosability Enhancements

Setup Automatic Diagnostic Repository

As mentioned earlier regarding the 11G changes to the Oracle flexible architecture, 11G has introduced the concept of the Automatic Diagnostic Repository (ADR). The ADR is a directory structure for diagnostic files such as traces, dumps, the alert log, health monitor reports, and more. The directory structure supports multiple instances and multiple Oracle products. Each instance of each product will store diagnostic data underneath its own home directory within the ADR. ADR provides a unified directory structure along with consistent diagnostic data formats across products and instances. This plus a unified set of tools enables diagnostic data to be correlated and analyzed across multiple Oracle products.

DIAGNOSTIC_DEST parameter

Because all diagnostic data, including the alert log, is stored in the ADR, the initialization parameters BACKGROUND_DUMP_DEST and USER_DUMP_DEST have been deprecated. They have been replaced by the initialization parameter DIAGNOSTIC_DEST. The DIAGNOSTIC_DEST parameter identifies the directory which serves as the ADR Base location

ADR Locations

The V$DIAG_INFO view lists all the important ADR locations for the current Oracle database instance. It also provides the number of active problems and incidents and the tracefiles for the current instance.

- **ADR Base** -- Path of ADR base
- **ADR Home** -- Path of ADR home for the current database instance
- **Diag Trace** -- Location of background process trace files, server process trace files, SQL trace files, and the text-formatted version of the alert log
- **Diag Alert** -- Location of the XML-formatted version of the alert log
- **Default Trace** -- File Path to the trace file for the current session
- **Diag Incident** -- File path for incident packages
- **Diag Cdump** -- Equivalent to cdump. Location for core dump files.
- **Health Monitor** -- Location for health monitor output.

```
SELECT name, value
FROM   v$diag_info;

NAME VALUE
-------------------- -----------------------------------------
Diag Enabled         TRUE
ADR Base             /u01/oracle
ADR Home             /u01/oracle/diag/rdbms/orcl/orcl
Diag Trace           /u01/oracle/diag/rdbms/orcl/orcl/trace
Diag Alert           /u01/oracle/diag/rdbms/orcl/orcl/alert
Diag Incident        /u01/oracle/diag/rdbms/orcl/orcl/incident
Diag Cdump           /u01/oracle/diag/rdbms/orcl/orcl/cdump
Health Monitor       /u01/oracle/diag/rdbms/orcl/orcl/hm
Default Trace File   /u01/oracle/diag/rdbms/orcl/orcl/trace/
                     orcl_ora_2245.trc
Active Problem Count 8
Active Incident Count 20
```

Use Support Workbench

Oracle Configuration Manager

The Support Workbench uses Oracle Configuration Manager (OCM) to upload diagnostic data to Oracle Support Services. If Oracle Configuration Manager is not installed or properly configured, the upload may fail. If this happens, a message is displayed with a request that you upload the file manually. You can upload manually through Oracle MetaLink.

Problems vs. Incidents

The fault diagnosability infrastructure in Oracle 11G introduces two concepts for the Oracle Database: problems and incidents. A problem is defined as a critical error in the database. Critical errors manifest as internal errors, such as ORA-00600, ORA-07445, or ORA-04031. Problems are tracked in the ADR using a problem key, which is a text string that describes the problem.

An incident is defined as a single occurrence of a problem. When a problem occurs multiple times, an incident is created for each occurrence. Oracle timestamps the incidents and tracks them in the ADR. Incidents are identified by a numeric incident ID, which is unique within the ADR. Each incident in the database generates the following actions:

- An entry is made in the alert log.
- An incident alert is sent to Oracle Enterprise Manager.
- Diagnostic data about the incident is stored in the form of dump files.
- One or more incident dumps are stored in the ADR in a subdirectory created for that incident.

Flood Control

A single problem could generate hundreds of incidents in a short period of time. If every action generated dumps as described above, this would generate a huge amount of diagnostic data. That much data would not aid diagnosis, would consume significant space in the ADR and could possibly slow down the process of diagnosing and resolving the problem. Oracle applies a flood control mechanism to incident generation to prevent this from happening. After certain thresholds are reached, incidents become flood-controlled. A flood-controlled incident generates an alert log entry, is recorded in the ADR, but does not generate incident dumps.

Threshold levels for incident flood control are predetermined and cannot be changed. They are defined as follows:

- After five incidents occur for the same problem key in one hour, subsequent incidents for this problem key are flood-controlled.
- After 25 incidents occur for the same problem key in one day, subsequent incidents for this problem key are flood-controlled.
- After 50 incidents for the same problem key occur in one hour, or 250 incidents for the same problem key occur in one day, subsequent incidents for the problem key are not recorded at all in the ADR. The database will write a message to the alert log indicating that no further incidents will be recorded.

The Automatic Diagnostic Repository has two distinct retention policies for incidents that determine how long data will be kept on disk from the time of the incident. The incident <u>metadata</u> retention policy determines how long the ADR will retain the metadata on incidents. It defaults to one year. The incident <u>files and dumps</u> retention policy sets the time that dump files will be kept. It is one month by default.

Incident Packaging Service

An incident package is a collection of metadata stored in the Automatic Diagnostic Repository which points to diagnostic data files and other files both related to a given incident. When creating a package, you select one or more problems to add to the package. The Support Workbench then adds associated problem information, incident information, and diagnostic files to the package. By default only the first and last three incidents for each problem are added to the package. Any incidents that are over 90 days old will not be included. After the package is created, you can add one or more external files, remove selected files, or edit selected files in the package to remove sensitive data. Only the package metadata is modified when performing any of these actions. When you are ready to upload the information to Oracle Support, you create a zip file that contains all the files referenced by the package metadata and upload the zip file through Oracle Configuration Manager. The Incident packaging service (IPS) is the tool which performs all of these steps. Because all diagnostic data in the ADR relating to a critical error are tagged with the incident number, the incident packaging service identifies them automatically and adds them to the zip file.

ADRCI

The Automatic Diagnostic Repository Command Interpreter (ADRCI) is a command-line utility that is part of the Oracle 11G fault diagnosability infrastructure. ADRCI's primary functions include:

- Viewing diagnostic data in the Automatic Diagnostic Repository.
- Viewing Health Monitor reports.
- Packaging incident and problem information for Oracle Support.

Diagnostic data viewable from within ADRCI includes incident and problem descriptions, trace files, dumps, health monitor reports, alert log entries, and more. ADRCI can be used in interactive mode or within scripts. ADRCI can also execute scripts of ADRCI commands just as SQL*Plus can execute scripts of SQL and PL/SQL commands. There is no login to ADRCI -- it is secured by OS-level file permissions only.

ADRCI HOMEPATH

An ADR home is the root directory for all diagnostic data for a particular instance of a given Oracle product or component. All ADR homes share the same hierarchical directory structure that starts at the ADR_BASE directory. Some ADRCI commands can work with multiple ADR homes simultaneously while others require that a single ADR home be set within ADRCI before issuing the command. The current ADRCI homepath determines the ADR homes that are searched for diagnostic data when an ADRCI command is issued. It does so by pointing to a specific directory within the ADR base hierarchy. When pointed to a single ADR home directory, that ADR home is the only current ADR home. If the homepath points to a higher directory, all ADR homes that are below the directory that is pointed to become current. The ADR homepath is null by default when ADRCI starts, which means that all the ADR homes beneath the ADR_BASE are current. The SHOW HOME and SHOW HOMEPATH commands display the current ADR homes. The SET HOMEPATH command sets the homepath to a specific directory.

Alert Log

Starting with Oracle 11g, the alert log is written as both an XML-formatted file and as a plain text file. You can view either format with any text editor. Alternately, you can use ADRCI to view the XML-formatted alert log with the XML tags stripped. By default, ADRCI displays the alert log in your default editor. You can use the SET EDITOR command to change the editor used by ADRCI.

Trace Files

You can use ADRCI to view the names of trace files that are currently in the ADR. You can view the names of all trace files, or a filtered subset of names. ADRCI has commands to obtain a list of trace files whose file name matches a search string, exist in a particular directory, pertain to a particular incident, or a combination of these. The SHOW TRACEFILE command displays a list of the files in the trace directory and in all incident directories under the current ADR home.

Show Incident

You can use the ADRCI SHOW INCIDENT command to display information about open incidents. For each incident, the incident ID, problem key, and incident creation time are shown. If the ADRCI homepath includes multiple current ADR homes, the report displays incidents from all of them.

```
SHOW INCIDENT
ADR Home =
/u03/app/oracle/product/11.1.0/db_2/log/diag/rdbms/orcl11g/orcl11g:
*************************************************************
INCIDENT_ID       PROBLEM_KEY                CREATE_TIME
----------------  -------------------------  ---------------------
4218              ORA 603                    2011-03-18
                                             21:35:49.322161 -07:00
4219              ORA 600 [4134]             2011-03-20
                                             21:35:47.862114 -07:00
4224              ORA 600 [4138]             2011-04-01
                                             21:35:25.012579 -07:00
3 rows fetched
```

The following are variations on the SHOW INCIDENT command:

```
SHOW INCIDENT -MODE BRIEF
SHOW INCIDENT -MODE DETAIL
SHOW INCIDENT -MODE DETAIL -P "INCIDENT_ID=1681"
```

Packaging Incidents with ADRCI

Packaging incidents is a three-step process:

1. Create a logical incident package.
2. Add diagnostic information to the incident package
3. Generate the physical incident package

You can use either Oracle Enterprise manager or ADRCI to perform incident packaging. Using ADRCI, the initial logical incident package is created with the **IPS CREATE PACKAGE** command. There are several variants of this command depending on what metadata you want added to the package. For example, **IPS CREATE PACKAGE INCIDENT incident_number** will create a package with metadata referencing ADR data for the specified incident number. **IPS CREATE PACKAGE PROBLEM problem_ID** will create a package and include diagnostic information for incidents that reference the specified problem ID. IPS **CREATE PACKAGE**

PROBLEMKEY "problem_key" will create a package with diagnostic information for incidents that reference the specified problem key. **IPS CREATE PACKAGE SECONDS sec** will create a package and include diagnostic information for all incidents that occurred from sec seconds ago until now. **IPS CREATE PACKAGE** with no additional information will create an empty package. You will need to add all incident data or files manually.

Once a package has been created (empty or not), you can add additional diagnostic information to it. You can add all diagnostic information for a particular incident, or individual named files within the ADR. To add an incident to an existing package, you would use the following command: **IPS ADD INCIDENT incident_number PACKAGE package_number**. To add a file, you would use the command: **IPS ADD FILE filespec PACKAGE package_number**. The file specification must be a fully qualified file name including the path. Only files that are within the ADR base directory hierarchy may be added.

Once the logical package has been created and any additional diagnostic data added, you create a physical package in the form of a zip file. To generate a physical incident package, you'll use the following command from within ADRCI: **IPS GENERATE PACKAGE package_number IN path**. This generates a complete physical package in the designated path as a zip file. The following command creates a physical package in the directory /home/george/oracle_support from logical package number 5: **IPS GENERATE PACKAGE 5 IN /home/george/oracle_support**. It is also possible to generate an incremental package. An incremental package will contain only the incidents that have occurred since the last package generation. To generate an incremental physical incident package, use the following command: **IPS GENERATE PACKAGE package_number IN path INCREMENTAL**.

Run health checks

Health Monitor

The Health Monitor framework is new with Oracle 11G. Health Monitor is part of the Database Fault Diagnosability Infrastructure and is designed for running diagnostic checks on the database. Health Monitor checks examine various layers and components of the database. Checks can detect file corruptions, physical and logical block corruptions, undo and redo corruptions, data dictionary corruptions, and more. The health checks generate findings reports and often recommendations for resolving problems. Health Monitor stores all findings, recommendations, and other information in the Automatic Diagnostic Repository. Health checks can be initiated reactively or manually.

- **Reactive** health checks are run automatically in response to a critical error.
- **Manual** health checks are run manually by the DBA using either the DBMS_HM PL/SQL package or the Enterprise Manager interface.

There are two modes for running health checks, DB-online and DB-offline:

- **DB-online** mode means the check can be run while the database is open or mounted.
- **DB-offline** mode means the check can be run when the instance is available but the database itself is in nomount mode.

All of the health checks can be run in DB-online mode. Only the Redo Integrity Check and the DB Structure Integrity Check can be used in DB-offline mode. The available Health Monitor checks are:

- **DB Structure Integrity Check** —- Verifies the integrity of database files and reports failures if these files are inaccessible, corrupt or inconsistent.

- **Data Block Integrity Check** —- Detects disk image block corruptions such as checksum failures, head/tail mismatch, and logical inconsistencies within the block. This check does not detect inter-block or inter-segment corruption.
- **Redo Integrity Check** —- Scans the contents of the redo log for accessibility and corruption, as well as the archive logs, if available.
- **Undo Segment Integrity Check** —- Finds logical undo corruptions. If it locates an undo corruption, it uses PMON and SMON to try to recover the corrupted transaction.
- **Transaction Integrity Check** —- This is identical to the Undo Segment Integrity Check except that it checks a single specific transaction.
- **Dictionary Integrity Check** —- Examines the integrity of core dictionary objects, such as tab$ and col$.

DBMS_HM Package

You can run health checks manually using either Oracle Enterprise manager or the DBMS_HM package. The DBMS_HM package has a procedure called RUN_CHECK that is used for running a health check. To call RUN_CHECK, supply the name of the check and a name for the run, as follows:

```
BEGIN
  DBMS_HM.RUN_CHECK('Dictionary Integrity Check',
'di_check');
END;
```

The available heath checks can be found in the V$HM_CHECK view. You can obtain a list of health check names with the following query:

```
SELECT  name
FROM    v$hm_check
WHERE   internal_check='N';

NAME
--------------------------------
DB Structure Integrity Check
Data Block Integrity Check
Redo Integrity Check
Transaction Integrity Check
Undo Segment Integrity Check
Dictionary Integrity Check
```

Most health checks have input parameters. The parameter names and descriptions are available in the V$HM_CHECK_PARAM view. Some of the parameters are mandatory and others are optional. When optional parameters are omitted, the default values are used. You can display parameter information for all health checks with the following query:

```
SELECT  c.name check_name, p.name parameter_name,
        p.type, p.default_value, p.description
FROM    v$hm_check_param p, v$hm_check c
WHERE   p.check_id = c.id and c.internal_check = 'N'
ORDER BY c.name;
```

You pass input parameters to the input_params argument of DBMS_HM.RUN_CHECK as name/value pairs separated by semicolons (;). The following example passes the transaction ID as a parameter to the Transaction Integrity Check:

```
BEGIN
DBMS_HM.RUN_CHECK (
check_name => 'Transaction Integrity Check',
run_name => 'hm_run',
input_params => 'TXN_ID=6.23.1');
```

Use SQL Repair Advisor

SRA Functionality

If a SQL statement fails with a critical error, the new SQL Repair Advisor may be able to repair the failed statement. When run against a failed statement, the advisor analyzes the statement to determine why it failed and can often recommend a patch to resolve the error. If applied, the SQL patch circumvents the failure by forcing the query optimizer to choose an alternate execution plan. SQL Repair Advisor is run from the Problem Details page of the Support Workbench in Oracle Enterprise Manager. What you'll need to know about SQL Repair advisor for the exam is that it is made to repair SQL statements that fail with a critical error. It is not made to tune functional statements. Also, implementing a patch does not change the SQL statement itself. The patch acts much like a SQL profile -- changing the execution plan chosen by the optimizer for the SQL statement as written.

Support Workbench

You can run the SQL Repair Advisor from the Problem Details page of the Support Workbench in Oracle Enterprise manager. If a SQL statement has failed with a critical error, a critical error will be present in the alerts section of OEM. The SQL Repair Advisor is available under the 'Problem Details' page for the displayed critical error.

DBMS_SQLDIAG

The SQL Repair Advisor can also be run by creating and executing a diagnostic task using the CREATE_DIAGNOSIS_TASK and EXECUTE_DIAGNOSIS_TASK of the SQLDIAG package. The SQL Repair Advisor reproduces the critical error and then tries to produce a SQL patch to work around the problem. The steps to diagnose and resolve a SQL patch are

1. Use DBMS_SQLDIAG.CREATE_DIAGNOSIS_TASK to create a new diagnosis task.
2. Use DBMS_SQLDIAG.EXECUTE_DIAGNOSIS_TASK with the task ID from step 1.
3. Use DBMS_SQLDIAG.REPORT_DIAGNOSIS_TASK to generate a report of the results.
4. Use DBMS_SQLDIAG.ACCEPT_SQL_PATCH to accept a patch.
5. Rerun the SQL statement to verify that it no longer fails.

Database Replay

Overview of Workload Capture

When to use Database Replay

Before making significant hardware or software upgrades to a production Oracle database, typically extensive testing is performed to verify the changes will not adversely affect the system. However, making such testing close enough to reality to provide a valid test is very difficult. Often problems are encountered after the upgrade that were not located during the testing period. There are various third-party tools on the market to provide load testing for Oracle, simulating the workload from multiple users. However, the workloads generated are not as complex and interactive as that generated by a real production system. Oracle 11G's new Database Replay feature enables system administrators to perform real-world testing by capturing the production database workload and replaying it on another database. In addition, it provides analysis and reporting of potential problems and recommend ways to resolve these problems.

What is captured by Database Replay

Oracle Database Replay captures all external database calls made to the system during the workload capture period. The capture includes all relevant information about the client request, such as SQL text, bind values, and transaction information. Background activities of the database and scheduler jobs are not captured. In addition, the following types of client requests are not captured in a workload:

- Direct path load of data from external files using utilities such as SQL*Loader
- Shared server requests (Oracle MTS)
- Oracle Streams
- Advanced replication streams
- Non-PL/SQL based Advanced Queuing (AQ)

- Flashback queries
- Oracle Call Interface (OCI) based object navigations
- Non SQL-based object access
- Distributed transactions

Using Workload capture and replay

Capturing the workload

It is a best practice to restart the database before capturing the production workload. This ensures that ongoing and dependent transactions are allowed to be completed or rolled back before the capture begins. If the database is not restarted before the capture, transactions that are in progress or have yet to be committed will be only partially captured in the workload.

Define Workload Filters

By default, all activities from all user sessions are recorded during workload capture. Workload filters can be used to include or exclude specific user sessions during the workload capture. You can use either inclusion filters or exclusion filters in a workload capture, but not both simultaneously. Inclusion filters specify user sessions that will be captured in the workload. Exclusion filters enable you to specify user sessions that will not be captured in the workload. To add filters to a workload capture, you use the **DBMS_WORKLOAD_CAPTURE.ADD_FILTER** procedure. To remove an existing filter, you use the **DBMS_WORKLOAD_CAPTURE.DELETE_FILTER** procedure.

Setting Up the Capture Directory

Before starting the workload capture, you must decide on the directory where the captured workload will be stored. Before starting the capture, verify that the directory is empty and has enough space for the workload. If the directory runs out of disk space during a workload capture, the capture will stop.

Starting a Workload Capture

You should have a well-defined starting point for the workload so that the database being used to replay the workload can be restored to the same point before starting the captured workload. It is best not to have any active user sessions when starting a workload capture. Active sessions may have ongoing transactions which will not be replayed completely. Consider restarting the database in RESTRICTED mode prior to starting the workload capture. When the workload capture begins, the database will automatically switch to UNRESTRICTED mode and normal operations can continue while the workload is being captured. You begin a workload capture using the procedure **DBMS_WORKLOAD_CAPTURE.START_CAPTURE**.

Stopping a Workload Capture

To stop a workload capture in progress, you use the **DBMS_WORKLOAD_CAPTURE.FINISH_CAPTURE** procedure.

Exporting AWR Data for Workload Capture

You can export AWR data from the production machine in order to enable detailed analysis of the workload on both systems. This data is required if you plan to run the AWR Compare Period report on a pair of workload captures or replays. To export AWR data, you use the **DBMS_WORKLOAD_CAPTURE.EXPORT_AWR** procedure.

Workload Capture Views

The following views allow you to monitor a workload capture. You can also use Oracle Enterprise Manager to monitor a workload capture:

- **DBA_WORKLOAD_CAPTURES** -- Lists all the workload captures that have been created in the current database.
- **DBA_WORKLOAD_FILTERS** -- Lists all workload filters used for workload captures defined in the current database.

Preparing the Replay

After the workload has been captured, the information, it's necessary to preprocess the capture files prior to using them in a replay. Preprocessing converts the captured data into replay files and creates the required metadata needed to replay the workload. After preprocessing the captured workload, it can be replayed multiple times on any replay system running the same version of Oracle. As a general rule, it's recommended to move the capture files to another system for preprocessing. While the capture itself has a minimal overhead, workload preprocessing can be time consuming and resource intensive. It is better that this step be performed on the test system where the workload will be replayed rather than on the production database. Capture files are processed using the **DBMS_WORKLOAD_REPLAY.PROCESS_CAPTURE** procedure.

Replaying the Workload

After you have preprocessed a captured workload, it can be replayed on the test system. In the workload replay, Oracle will perform the actions recorded during the workload capture. It will re-create all captured external client requests with the same timing, concurrency, and transaction dependencies that occurred on the production system. Database Replay uses a program called the replay client to re-create the external client requests. You may need to use multiple replay clients depending on the scope of the captured workload. The reply client has an imbedded calibration tool to help determine the number of replay clients required for a given workload. The entire workload from the production database is replayed. This includes DML and SQL queries, so the data in the replay system must be as logically similar to the data in the capture system as possible. Ensuring the systems are as identical as possible will minimize data divergence and enable a more reliable analysis of the replay. Replaying a database workload requires the following steps:

Setting Up the Replay Directory

The captured workload must have been preprocessed and copied to the replay system. An Oracle directory object for the directory to which the preprocessed workload has been copied must exist in the replay system.

Resolving References to External Systems

A captured workload may contain references to external systems, such as database links or external tables. These should be reconfigured to avoid impacting production systems during replay. External references that need to be resolved before replaying a workload include: Database links, external tables, directory objects, URLs, and e-mail addresses. If these external connections are not changed before starting the replay, you could end up changing data in production systems, sending emails to users, and other undesirable actions.

Remapping Connections

Connection strings used to connect to the production system are captured in the workload. You must remap these connection strings to the replay system for the replay to succeed. The replay clients can then connect to the replay system using the remapped connections. For Oracle Real

Application Cluster databases, you can map all connection strings to a load balancing connection string.

Specifying Replay Options

There are several options that determine the behavior of the database replay.

- **synchronization** -- determines whether the COMMIT order will be preserved during replay. By default, synchronization is enabled. All transactions will be executed only after all dependent transactions have been committed. If you disable this option, the replay will likely have significant data divergence. This may not be a problem if the workload consists primarily of independent transactions. Not preserving the commit order can also lead to a faster replay, if 'stress testing' of the replay system is desirable.
- **connect_time_scale** -- enables you to scale the elapsed time between the time when the sessions connected to the database during the workload capture began and when each session connects during the replay. This option allows you to manipulate the session connect time during replay with a given percentage value. By default, the value is 100, which will attempt to connect all sessions as captured. Setting this parameter to 0 will attempt to connect all sessions immediately.
- **think_time_scale** -- allows you to scale user think time during replay. User think time is the elapsed time while the replayed user waits between issuing calls within a single session. A value of 100 means that time between calls will be the same as they were during the capture. A value of zero will eliminate all wait time between calls.
- **think_time_auto_correct** -- If user calls are being executed slower during replay than during capture, you can make the database replay attempt to catch up by setting this parameter to TRUE. When set to true, it will make the replay client shorten the think

time between calls, so that the overall elapsed time of the replay will more closely match the captured elapsed time.

Setting Up Replay Clients

The replay client is a multithreaded program where each thread submits a workload from a captured session. It is an executable file named **wrc** located in the $ORACLE_HOME/bin directory. The replay user that wrc logs in as needs the DBA role and cannot be SYS. The wrc executable uses the following syntax:

```
wrc [user/pword[@server]] MODE=[value] [keyword=[value]]
```

The mode parameter specifies the action to be taken when the wrc executable is run. Possible values include replay (the default), calibrate, and list_hosts. The parameter keyword specifies the options to use for the execution and is dependent on the mode selected. To display the possible keywords and their corresponding values, run the wrc executable without any arguments.

The modes that you can select when running the wrc executable and their corresponding keywords are:

- **replay** (the default) -- runs a captured workload. In replay mode, the wrc executable accepts the following keywords:
    - ✓ **userid and password** -- specify the user ID and password of a replay user for the replay client. If unspecified, the user ID defaults to the SYSTEM user.
    - ✓ **server** -- specifies the connection string that is used to connect to the replay system. If unspecified, the value defaults to an empty string.
    - ✓ **replaydir** -- specifies the directory that contains the preprocessed workload capture you want to replay. If unspecified, it defaults to the current directory.
    - ✓ **debug** -- specifies whether debug data will be created.

- ✓ **workdir** -- specifies the directory where the client logs will be written. This parameter is only used in conjunction with the debug parameter.
- ✓ **connection_override** -- specifies whether to override the connection mappings stored in the DBA_WORKLOAD_CONNECTION_MAP view.
- **calibrate** -- causes wrc to return an estimate of the number of replay clients and hosts that are required to replay a particular workload. In calibration mode, wrc accepts the following keywords:
  - ✓ **replaydir** -- specifies the directory that contains the preprocessed workload capture. It defaults to the current directory.
  - ✓ **process_per_cpu** -- specifies the maximum number of client processes that can run per CPU. The default value is 4.
  - ✓ **threads_per_process** -- specifies the maximum number of threads that can run within a client process. The default value is 50.
- **list_hosts** -- Displays the hosts that participated in a workload capture and workload replay. In list_hosts mode, the wrc executable accepts only one keyword:
  - ✓ **replaydir** -- specifies the directory that contains the preprocessed workload capture you want to replay. If unspecified, it defaults to the current directory

Analysis and Reporting

Once the workload replay has completed, in-depth reporting is available so that you can perform detailed analysis of both the workload capture and the replay operation. The summary report provides basic information such as errors encountered during replay and data divergence in rows returned by DML or SQL queries. A comparison of several statistics between the source and replay servers is also provided. You can use Automatic Workload Repository reports for advanced analysis of the workload processing between the two servers.

Using the Data Recovery Advisor

Overview of Data Recovery Advisor

Functions of the DRA

Oracle's Data Recovery Advisor is a data corruption repair function integrated with Support Workbench, database health checks and RMAN. It can display data corruption problems, assess their extent and impact, recommend repair options, and automate the repair process. In the context of Data Recovery Advisor, a health check is a diagnostic procedure run by the Health Monitor to assess the state of the database or its components. Health checks are invoked reactively when an error occurs and can also be invoked manually.

Failures

A failure is a persistent data corruption detected by a health check. They are usually detected reactively when a database operation encounters corrupted data and generates an error. This will automatically invoke a health check in the database. The check will search the database for failures related to the error and record any findings in the Automatic Diagnostic Repository. Data Recovery Advisor can generate repair advice and repair failures only after failures have been detected by the database and stored in the ADR. Data Recovery Advisor can report on and repair failures such as inaccessible files, physical and logical block corruptions, and I/O failures. All failures are assigned a priority: CRITICAL, HIGH, or LOW, and a status of OPEN or CLOSED.

- **CRITICAL** priority failures require immediate attention because they make the whole database unavailable. Typically, critical failures bring down the instance and are diagnosed during the subsequent startup.

- **HIGH** priority failures make a database partially unavailable or unrecoverable, and usually have to be repaired in a reasonably short time.
- **LOW** priority indicates that failures can be ignored until more important failures are fixed.

Repairs

Data Recovery Advisor allows you to view repair options. Repairs might involve the use of block media recovery, datafile media recovery, or Oracle Flashback Database. In general, Data Recovery Advisor presents both automated and manual repair options. If appropriate, you can choose an automated repair option in order to perform a repair. In an automated repair, Data Recovery Advisor performs the repair, verifies the repair success, and closes the relevant failures.

Repairing data failures using DRA

The recommended workflow for repairing data failures from RMAN is to run the following commands in sequence during an RMAN session: **LIST FAILURE** to display failures, **ADVISE FAILURE** to display repair options, and **REPAIR FAILURE** to fix the failures.

LIST FAILURE

The LIST FAILURE command displays failures against which you can run the ADVISE FAILURE and REPAIR FAILURE commands.

```
RMAN> LIST FAILURE;
List of Database Failures
=========================
Failure ID Priority Status Time Detected Summary
---------- -------- ------ ------------- -------
274        HIGH     OPEN   12-APR-11     One or more non-system
datafiles are missing
329        HIGH     OPEN   12-APR-11     Datafile 1:
'/u01/oradata/prod/system01.dbf'
                                         contains one or more
corrupt blocks
```

ADVISE FAILURE

Use the ADVISE FAILURE command to display repair options for the specified failures. This command prints a summary of the failures identified by the Data Recovery Advisor and implicitly closes all open failures that are already fixed. The ADVISE FAILURE command indicates the repair strategy that Data Recovery Advisor considers optimal for a given set of failures. Data Recovery Advisor verifies repair feasibility before proposing a repair strategy. For example, it will check that all backups and archived redo log files needed for media recovery are available. It can generate both manual and automated repair options.

```
RMAN> ADVISE FAILURE;
List of Database Failures
=========================
Failure ID Priority Status Time Detected Summary
---------- -------- ------ ------------- -------
274        HIGH     OPEN   12-APR-11     One or more non-system
datafiles are missing
329        HIGH     OPEN   12-APR-11     Datafile 1:
'/u01/oradata/prod/system01.dbf'
                                         contains one or more corrupt
blocks

analyzing automatic repair options; this may take some time
using channel ORA_DISK_1
analyzing automatic repair options complete

Mandatory Manual Actions
========================
no manual actions available

Optional Manual Actions
=======================
1. If file /u01/oradata/prod/data01.dbf was unintentionally renamed
or moved, restore it

Automated Repair Options
========================
Option Repair Description
------ ------------------
1      Restore and recover datafile 31; Perform block media recovery
of block 43481 in file 1

Strategy: The repair includes complete media recovery with no data
loss
Repair script:
/u01/oracle/log/diag/rdbms/prod/prod/hm/reco_740113269.hm
```

CHANGE FAILURE

The CHANGE FAILURE command allows you to change the failure priority from HIGH to LOW or the reverse. You cannot change to or from CRITICAL priority.

```
RMAN> CHANGE FAILURE 3 PRIORITY LOW;
```

REPAIR FAILURE

The REPAIR FAILURE command is used to repair database failures identified by the Data Recovery Advisor. The target database instance must be started, it must be a single-instance database and cannot be a physical standby database. It is important that at most one RMAN session is running the REPAIR FAILURE command. The only exception is REPAIR FAILURE ... PREVIEW, which is permitted in concurrent RMAN sessions. To perform an automated repair, the Data Recovery Advisor may require specific backups and archived redo logs. If the files are not available, then the recovery will not be possible. Data Recovery Advisor consolidates repairs whenever possible so that a single repair can fix multiple failures. If one has not yet been issued in the current RMAN session, REPAIR FAILURE performs an implicit ADVISE FAILURE. RMAN always verifies that failures are still relevant and automatically closes failures that have already been repaired. After executing a repair, RMAN reevaluates all open failures on the chance that some of them may also have been fixed.

Perform proactive health checks

VALIDATE DATABASE

The VALIDATE DATABASE command validates all datafiles and control files, checking for corrupt blocks and missing files. If the database is currently using a server parameter file, then RMAN validates this file as well. By default, the VALIDATE command checks for physical corruption only. In a physical corruption, the database does not recognize the block at all. In a logical corruption, the contents of the block are logically inconsistent. You can specify CHECK LOGICAL to check for logical corruption. RMAN populates the V$DATABASE_ BLOCK_CORRUPTION view with its findings. Block corruptions can be divided into interblock corruption and intrablock corruption. In intrablock corruption, the corruption occurs within the block itself and can be either physical or logical corruption. In interblock corruption, the corruption occurs between blocks and can only be logical corruption. The VALIDATE command has the ability to check for intrablock corruptions only.

Health Monitor

Health Monitor provides two ways to run health checks proactively:

1. Using the DBMS_HM PL/SQL package. The DBMS_HM procedure for running a health check is called RUN_CHECK. To call RUN_CHECK, supply the name of the check and a name for the run:

    ```
    BEGIN
    DBMS_HM.RUN_CHECK('Dictionary Integrity Check',
                     'proactive_check');
    END;
    ```

2. Using the Enterprise Manager interface, found on the Checkers subpage of the Advisor Central page

Security: New Features

Changes to Oracle Passwords

Oracle Database has added several enhancements to password security in 11G. Among them, you now have the following new features:

- The ability to locate standard accounts using default passwords.
- Enforced case sensitivity for database accounts by default.
- A password complexity verification function.
- Stronger password hashing algorithm.

Locating accounts with default passwords

In Oracle Database 11g Release 1, most of the default accounts are locked and have their passwords expired at database creation. However, if you have upgraded from an earlier release, there may be unlocked user accounts such as HR, OE, and SCOTT that are not locked and have default passwords. To improve database security, the passwords on these accounts should be changed. Failing to do so can make your database vulnerable to attacks. To find both locked and unlocked accounts that use default passwords, query the DBA_USERS_WITH_DEFPWD view from an account with SYSDBA privileges.

```
SELECT  d.username, u.account_status
FROM    dba_users_with_defpwd d,
        dba_users u
WHERE   d.username = u.username;

USERNAME   ACCOUNT_STATUS
---------  -------------------
SCOTT      EXPIRED & LOCKED
```

Case-sensitive Passwords

New with Oracle 11G, user account passwords are case sensitive by default. You can alter this behavior using the SEC_CASE_SENSITIVE_LOGON initialization parameter. Only users with the ALTER SYSTEM privilege can alter the value of this parameter. Set it to TRUE to enable case sensitivity or FALSE to disable case sensitivity. Oracle strongly recommends that you leave case sensitivity in passwords enabled.

Passwords were not case sensitive in previous releases of Oracle Database. If you import user accounts from a previous release into Oracle 11G, the passwords in these accounts remain case insensitive until the user changes his or her password from within 11G. This is also the case if you upgrade from an earlier release of Oracle to 11G. When the password of a user account from the previous release is changed, it will become case sensitive (assuming that SEC_CASE_SENSITIVE_LOGON is set to TRUE). You can find users who have case sensitive or case insensitive passwords by querying the DBA_USERS view. The new PASSWORD_VERSIONS column in this view indicates the release in which the password was created.

```
SELECT  username, password_versions
FROM    dba_users

USERNAME                PASSWORD_VERSIONS
------------------      -----------------
SMITH                   10G 11G
RICHARDS                10G 11G
HARVEY                  11G
ROONEY                  10G
```

The passwords for accounts SMITH, and RICHARDS were originally created in Release 10g and were then reset in Release 11g. Their passwords, assuming case sensitivity has been enabled, are now case sensitive, as is the password for HARVEY, which was originally created in 11G. However, the account for ROONEY is still using the Release 10g standard, so it is case insensitive.

The account passwords in the Oracle password file will also be case-sensitive by default. You can control the case-sensitivity of the password file by using the IGNORECASE parameter when creating the password file with orapwd. By default, IGNORECASE is set to N, which means that passwords are treated as case-sensitive.

```
orapwd file=orapw entries=100 ignorecase=y
```

Password Complexity Verification

Oracle supplies a basic password complexity verification function with 11G called VERIFY_FUNCTION_11G. The function is created by running the UTLPWDMG.SQL script. You can customize this function to meet your own requirements. Oracle recommends that you do so, in fact. By default, password complexity verification is not enabled. To enable password complexity verification you must perform the following steps:

- Log in to SQL*Plus with administrative privileges and run the UTLPWDMG.SQL script (or your variant thereof) to create the password complexity function in the SYS schema.
- In the default profile or the user profile, set the PASSWORD_VERIFY_FUNCTION setting to either the sample password complexity function in the UTLPWDMG.SQL script, or to your customized function. Use one of the following methods:
    - ✓ Log in to SQL*Plus with administrator privileges and use the CREATE PROFILE or ALTER PROFILE statement to enable the function.
      ```
      ALTER PROFILE default LIMIT
        PASSWORD_VERIFY_FUNCTION verify_function_11G;
      ```
    - ✓ In Oracle Enterprise Manager, go to the Edit Profiles page and then under Complexity, select the name of the password complexity function from the Complexity function list.

Stronger password hashing algorithm

Oracle 11G can make use of a cryptographic hashing algorithm based on SHA-1. This helps protect against password-based security threats by including support for mixed case characters, special characters, and multibyte characters in passwords. The SHA-1 hashing algorithm also adds salt to each password when it is hashed, which provides additional protection.

Encrypt a tablespace

Overview

It is possible to encrypt any permanent tablespace to protect sensitive data. Tablespace encryption is transparent to database users and your applications. Encrypted tablespaces are designed protect your data from unauthorized access by means <u>other</u> than through the database. This would include events such as someone getting hold of backup tapes of your database. Encrypted tablespaces also protect data from users who try to access database files directly through the operating system. When a tablespace is encrypted, all tablespace blocks are encrypted. All segment types are supported for encryption, including tables, clusters, indexes, LOBs, table and index partitions, and so on. To maximize security, data from an encrypted tablespace is automatically encrypted when written to the undo tablespace, to the redo logs, and to any temporary tablespace. There is no disk space overhead for encrypting a tablespace. The following statement creates an encrypted tablespace with the default encryption algorithm:

```
CREATE TABLESPACE secure_ts
DATAFILE '/u02/app/oracle/oradata/orcl11g/secure01.dbf' SIZE
200M
ENCRYPTION
DEFAULT STORAGE(ENCRYPT);
```

Oracle Wallet

Tablespace encryption uses the transparent data encryption feature of Oracle Database. This feature requires that you create an Oracle Wallet to store the master encryption key for the database. The wallet must be open before you can create the encrypted tablespace and before you can store or retrieve encrypted data. When you open the wallet, it is available to all sessions. It remains open until you explicitly close it or until the database is shut down.

Encryption Algorithms

Transparent data encryption supports industry-standard encryption algorithms, including the following: 3DES168, AES128, AES192, AES256. The encryption key length is implied by the algorithm name. For example, the AES128 algorithm uses 128-bit keys. You specify the algorithm to use when you create the tablespace, and different tablespaces in the same database can use different algorithms. While longer key lengths theoretically provide greater security, there is a trade-off in CPU overhead. AES128 is the default encryption algorithm.

Restrictions

- You cannot encrypt an existing tablespace with an ALTER TABLESPACE statement.
- Encrypted tablespaces are subject to restrictions when transporting to another database.
- When recovering a database with encrypted tablespaces you must open the Oracle wallet that contains the encryption key after database mount and before database open, so the recovery process can decrypt data blocks and redo.

Configure fine-grained access

Network Services

The Oracle database contains a set of PL/SQL utility packages, such as UTL_TCP, UTL_SMTP, UTL_MAIL, UTL_HTTP, and UTL_INADDR, which are designed to enable database users to access network services from within the database. In a default database installation, these packages are created with EXECUTE privileges granted to PUBLIC users. Prior to Oracle 11G, this meant that any user with access to an Oracle account also gained access to all of these network services. This release enhances the security of these packages by allowing database administrators the ability to restrict access to these packages.

Creating Access Control Lists

To configure fine-grained access to external network services, you create an access control list (ACL), which is stored in Oracle XML DB. It's possible to create the access control list by using Oracle XML DB itself, or by using the DBMS_NETWORK_ACL_ADMIN and DBMS_NETWORK_ACL_UTILITY PL/SQL packages.

To create the access control list by using the DBMS_NETWORK_ACL_ADMIN package, follow these steps:

1. Create the Access Control List and Its Privilege Definitions via the DBMS_NETWORK_ACL_ADMIN.CREATE_ACL procedure.

```
BEGIN
  DBMS_NETWORK_ACL_ADMIN.CREATE_ACL (
    acl          => 'file_name.xml',
    description  => 'file description',
    principal    => 'user_or_role',
    is_grant     => TRUE|FALSE,
    privilege    => 'connect|resolve',
    start_date   => null|timestamp_with_time_zone,
    end_date     => null|timestamp_with_time_zone);
END;
```

- **acl** -- a name for the access control list XML file.
- **description** -- a brief description of the purpose of this file.
- **principal** -- the initial user account or role being granted or denied permissions.
- **is_grant** -- either TRUE or FALSE, to indicate whether the privilege is to be granted or denied
- **privilege** -- either connect or resolve. Connect grants permission to connect to a network service. Resolve grants the user permission to resolve a network host name or an IP address.
- **start_date** --(Optional) starting date that the entry will be valid.
- **end_date** --(Optional) ending date that the entry will be valid.

2. Add additional users or roles to the access control list, or grant additional privileges to one user or role, via the DBMS_NETWORK_ACL_ADMIN.ADD_PRIVILEGE procedure.

```
BEGIN
  DBMS_NETWORK_ACL_ADMIN.ADD_PRIVILEGE (
    acl => 'file_name.xml',
    principal => 'user_or_role',
    is_grant => TRUE|FALSE,
    privilege => 'connect|resolve',
    position => null|value,
    start_date => null|timestamp_with_time_zone,
    end_date => null|timestamp_with_time_zone);
END;
```

The matching parameters that exist in ADD_PRIVILEGE and CREATE_ACL have the same meaning. The only new parameter is position, which sets the precedence for multiple users or roles.

3. Assign the access control list to one or more network host computers using the DBMS_NETWORK_ACL_ADMIN.ASSIGN_ACL procedure. Only one access control list can be assigned to any host computer, domain, or IP subnet, and if specified, the TCP port range. When you assign a new access control list to a network target, Oracle Database unassigns the previous access control list that was assigned to the same target.

```
BEGIN
  DBMS_NETWORK_ACL_ADMIN.ASSIGN_ACL (
    acl => 'file_name.xml',
    host => 'network_host',
    lower_port => null|port_number,
    upper_port => null|port_number);
END;
```

- **acl** --the name of the access control list XML file to assign to the network host.
- **host** -- the network host to which this access control list will be assigned. This setting can be a name or IP address of the network host, or you can enter localhost.
- **lower_port** -- (Optional) For TCP connections, enter the lower boundary of the port range. Use this setting for the connect

privilege only; omit it for the resolve privilege. The default is null, which means that there is no port restriction (that is, the ACL applies to all ports).
- **upper_port** -- (Optional) For TCP connections, enter the upper boundary of the port range. Use this setting for connect privileges only; omit it for resolve privileges. The default is null, which means that there is no port restriction (that is, the ACL applies to all ports).

Oracle SecureFiles

Use Secure File LOBS to store documents

SecureFile LOBs vs. BasicFile LOBs

In Oracle 11G, a new type of Large-Object storage has been added, SecureFile LOBs. The legacy LOB format has been renamed to BasicFile LOBs. SecureFile LOBs add several new capabilities to LOB data storage:

- Intelligent LOB compression enables users to explicitly compress data to save disk space.
- Intelligent LOB encryption allows encrypted data to be stored in-place and is available for random reads and writes.
- The deduplication option allows Oracle to automatically detect duplicate LOB data and conserve space by only storing a single copy of the data.
- LOB data path optimization includes logical cache above storage layer, read prefetching, new caching modes, vectored IO, and more.

db_securefile parameter

The new init.ora parameter, db_securefile, is used to determine the behavior of the Oracle database in reference to using or not using SecureFile LOBs or BasicFile LOBs. The possible values of this parameter are: ALWAYS, FORCE, PERMITTED, NEVER, and IGNORE. The meaning of each of the values is:

- **ALWAYS** -- attempt to create SecureFile LOBs but fall back to BasicFile LOBs if the tablespace is not using ASSM.
- **FORCE** -- force all LOBs created going forward to be SecureFile LOBs. If the LOB is being created in an MSSM tablespace, an error will be thrown.
- **PERMITTED** -- allow SecureFile LOBs to be created
- **NEVER** -- disallow SecureFile LOBs from being created. If a DML statement tries to create a column as a SecureFile LOB, it will

instead be created as a BasicFile LOB. If any SecureFile specific storage options or features are in the DML, an exception is created.
- **IGNORE** -- disallow SecureFile LOBs and ignore any errors that would otherwise be caused by forcing BasicFile LOBs with SecureFile options.

Migration to Secure File LOBs

Online redefinition is the only method Oracle recommends for migrating BasicFile LOBs to SecureFile LOBs. Online redefinition can be performed at the table or partition level. Using online redefinition means that the tables or partitions do not need to be taken offline. You can also perform the operation in parallel. However, the operation will require additional storage equal to the entire table or partition and all LOB segments. Also, after the migration, global indexes for the table will have to be rebuilt.

Use APIs to access Secure File LOBS

DBMS_LOB

SecureFiles inherit the LOB column settings for deduplication, encryption, and compression that were specified at the time the LOB was created. You can use the new procedures added to the DBMS_LOB package to determine or override the inherited values.

- **DBMS_LOB.GETOPTIONS** -- The current settings of a SecureFile LOB can be obtained using this function. An integer corresponding to a pre-defined constant based on the option type is returned. As an example, the value for DEDUPLICATE_OFF is 0. You won't need to know the values for the test. You might need to know the procedure name.
- **DBMS_LOB.SETOPTIONS** -- This procedure sets features of a SecureFile LOB (compression, deduplication, and encryption). It enables the features to be set on a per-LOB basis, overriding the default LOB settings.

- **DBMS_LOB.ISSECUREFILE** -- This function returns TRUE or FALSE depending on whether the LOB locator (BLOB or CLOB) passed to it is for a SecureFile.

DBMS_SPACE.SPACE_USAGE

The existing SPACE_USAGE procedure is overloaded to return information about LOB space usage. It returns the amount of disk space in blocks used by all the LOBs in the LOB segment. This procedure can only be used on tablespaces that are created with auto segment space management.

Miscellaneous New Features

Enhanced online table redefinition

Fewer exclusive Locks

Oracle Database provides a mechanism called online table redefinition to make table structure modifications without significantly affecting its availability. When a table is redefined online, it is accessible to both queries and DML during much of the redefinition process. Only during a very small window is the table is locked in the exclusive mode. The window is independent of the size of the table and complexity of the redefinition. Other than the period during which the table must be locked, the redefinition is transparent to users. In Oracle 11G, there have been enhancements to the online table redefinition process that have reduced the impact even further.

- In previous releases, a table could not be redefined if it had a log or materialized views defined. With Oracle 11G, this restriction has been lifted.
- Oracle 11G has eliminated the need for DML-blocking locks when creating or rebuilding an online index. Online index creation and rebuild prior to 11G required a DML-blocking lock at the beginning and end of the rebuild for a short period of time. This lock is no longer required, making these online index operations fully transparent.
- If a table redefinition does not logically affect PL/SQL packages that reference the table, recompilation is not needed. This reduces the time and effort to manually recompile dependent PL/SQL objects after an online table redefinition. This feature extends to views, synonyms, and other table dependent objects (with the exception of triggers) that are not logically affected by the redefinition.

Enhanced finer grained dependencies

In previous releases, metadata recorded mutual dependencies between objects with the granularity of the whole object. For example, View X depended on Table Y, or PL/SQL Procedure A depended on PL/SQL procedure B. If anything changed in the object that was referenced by a dependency, the object with the dependency was invalidated. This occurred even when the change in the dependent object created no logical requirement for the invalidation. For example, if a view referenced columns one through four on a table, and a fifth column was added to the table, the view would be invalidated despite there being no logical reason to do so. Oracle Database 11g records dependency metadata at a finer level of granularity so that the addition of another column would not invalidate the view. The increased granularity extends to PL/SQL dependencies. This feature benefits both the development and production environments. It's especially helpful when Oracle Database patchsets are applied because changes to schema objects are required to be compatible and thus won't generate consequential invalidations.

The notable exception to the rule is that of triggers on tables. When a table that a trigger is dependent on changes, the trigger will always be invalidated, regardless of logical dependencies. The trigger will be revalidated automatically the next time it is invoked.

Use Enhanced DDL

Waits for DDL operations

In order to work properly, data definition language (DDL) commands require exclusive locks on internal structures. At the time a DDL command is issued, there might be DML operations against the target object. If so, an exclusive lock won't be immediately available, and will cause the DDL statement to fail. This happens even though the DDL could have possibly succeeded if the command had been issued a second later. In Oracle 11G, this can be resolved by setting the WAIT option in the

DDL_LOCK_TIMEOUT initialization parameter. The wait time is specified instance-wide in the initialization parameter file, but can be modified at the session level. The WAIT option provides more flexibility to define grace periods for DDL commands to succeed. To specify a DDL lock timeout, the DDL_LOCK_TIMEOUT parameter must be set to an integer value that sets the number of seconds a DDL statement will wait for an exclusive lock. The permissible range of values for DDL_LOCK_TIMEOUT is 0 to 100,000. The default is 0. You can set DDL_LOCK_TIMEOUT at the system level using an ALTER SYSTEM statement, or at the session level with an ALTER SESSION statement.

Use Query and PL/SQL Result Cache

How the cache works

In Oracle 11G, a separate shared memory pool called the Result Cache Memory is now available. The result cache stores the results of SQL queries and PL/SQL functions. When these queries and functions are executed repeatedly, the results are retrieved directly from the cache resulting in a faster response time. The cached results are automatically invalidated when data in the dependent database objects is modified. The Result Cache Memory pool consists of the SQL Query Result Cache, which stores the results of SQL queries, and the PL/SQL Function Result Cache, which stores the values returned by PL/SQL functions. Query results that are bigger than the available space in the result cache will not be cached.

The use of the SQL query result cache can be controlled by setting the **RESULT_CACHE_MODE** initialization parameter. The possible values are **MANUAL** and **FORCE**. When set to MANUAL, you must use the **result_cache** hint in a SQL Query for its results to be cached.

```
SELECT /*+ result_cache */ deptno, AVG(sal)
FROM    emp
GROUP BY deptno;
```

If the result is not already available in the cache, then the query will be executed and the result stored in the cache. Subsequent executions of the statement (including the result cache hint) will use results from the cache. When the RESULT_CACHE_MODE parameter is set to FORCE, all SQL results use the cache by default. Using the **no_result_cache** hint in SQL statements will bypass the cache when using the FORCE mode.

```
SELECT /*+ no_result_cache */ deptno, AVG(sal)
FROM    emp
GROUP BY deptno;
```

You cannot cache results when you use the following database objects or functions in your SQL query:

- Dictionary and temporary tables
- Sequence CURRVAL and NEXTVAL pseudo columns
- SQL functions current_date, current_timestamp, local_timestamp, sys_guid, sysdate, and sys_timestamp
- Non-deterministic PL/SQL functions

Parameterized cache results can be reused if the query is equivalent and the parameter values are the same. Cached results are parameterized with the parameter values if any of the following constructs are used in the query:

- Bind variables.
- The following SQL functions: dbtimezone, uid, user, and sessiontimezone.
- NLS parameters.

Result Cache Parameters

- **RESULT_CACHE_MAX_SIZE** -- allows you to change the memory allocated to the result cache. The result cache is disabled if you set the value to 0 during database startup.

- **RESULT_CACHE_MAX_RESULT** -- specifies the maximum percentage of result cache memory that can be used by any single result. The default value is 5%, but you can specify any percent value between 1 and 100.
- **RESULT_CACHE_REMOTE_EXPIRATION** -- specifies the time (in minutes) for which a result that accesses remote database objects remains valid. When set to 0 (the default), the SQL query result cache is disabled for queries that access remote tables. Note that when you use a non-zero value, a DML on the remote database will not invalidate the result cache.

DBMS_RESULT_CACHE

The DBMS_RESULT_CACHE package allows the DBA to administer the portion of the shared pool used by the SQL and PL/SQL function result caches. Both these caches use the same infrastructure so DBMS_RESULT_CACHE operations affect both caches simultaneously. The DBMS_RESULT_CACHE package can be used to perform various operations such as bypassing the cache, retrieving statistics on the cache memory usage, and flushing the cache.

- **DBMS_RESULT_CACHE.BYPASS** -- sets the bypass mode for the Result Cache. When bypass mode is turned on, cached results are no longer used and no new results are saved. When bypass mode is turned off, the cache resumes normal operation.
- **DBMS_RESULT_CACHE.FLUSH** -- attempts to remove all the objects from the Result Cache, and depending on the arguments retains or releases the memory and retains or clears the statistics. Prior to flushing the cache, you should set BYPASS to ON.
- **DBMS_RESULT_CACHE.INVALIDATE** -- invalidates all the result-set objects that are dependent upon the specified dependency object.
- **DBMS_RESULT_CACHE.MEMORY_REPORT** -- produces a memory usage report for the Result Cache.

Client Result Cache

In addition to the server result cache, there is a new client result cache in 11G. The client-side result cache is completely separate from the server-side result cache. Unlike the server result cache, the OCI result cache does not cache results in the server SGA but rather in the memory of the client computer. The following server initialization parameters manager the client result cache:

- **CLIENT_RESULT_CACHE_SIZE** -- sets the memory allocated to the result cache. If you set the value to 0 (the default value), the result cache will be disabled.
- **CLIENT_RESULT_CACHE_LAG** -- sets the lag time for the client result cache. If the OCI application accesses the database infrequently, setting this parameter to a low value results in more round trips from the OCI client library to the database to keep the client result cache synchronized with the database.

Views

The following views provide information regarding the result cache:

- **V$RESULT_CACHE_STATISTICS** -- Lists the various cache settings and memory usage statistics.
- **V$RESULT_CACHE_MEMORY** -- Lists all the memory blocks and the corresponding statistics.
- **V$RESULT_CACHE_OBJECTS** -- Lists all the objects (cached results and dependencies) along with their attributes.
- **V$RESULT_CACHE_DEPENDENCY** -- Lists the dependency details between the cached results and dependencies.

Adaptive Cursor Sharing

Cursor sharing and Bind Peeking

Using bind variables in queries allows for the most effective use of server memory, as a single cursor can be created for a given SQL statement and then shared multiple times even as the values of the bind variables change. However, when bind variables are used against columns containing skewed data, the execution plan created for the original cursor can be less than optimal. This happens because the optimizer 'peeks' at the value of the bind variable(s) during the initial hard parse of the SQL statement. The values presented to the optimizer on the first statement are treated as representative of all subsequent values. In Oracle 11G, the concept of Adaptive Cursor Sharing has been implemented to resolve this issue. Adaptive Cursor Sharing allows the server to compare the effectiveness of execution plans between SQL statements with different bind variable values. If it detects suboptimal plans, it allows for the use of alternate execution plans for the same statement. This functionality is always enabled and neither requires nor allows any configuration. There are two concepts regarding Adaptive Cursor Sharing that you must be aware of for the exam.

Adapting to Bind Variables

- **Bind-Sensitive** -- Cursors where the optimizer has determined the optimal execution plan is dependent on the bind values are tagged as bind-sensitive.
- **Bind-Aware** -- Bind-sensitive cursors for which the optimizer has created alternate execution plans dependant on the bind values are tagged as Bind-Aware.

Temporary Tablespace Enhancements

Shrinking Temporary Tablespaces

When large sort operations are performed by the database, they can result in a temporary tablespace growing and occupying a considerable amount of disk space. When the sort operation completes, the extra space does not get released automatically to the file system; it is just marked as free and available for reuse. An unusually large sort operation might create a temporary tablespace much larger than what is required for normal operations. In 11G, a new command enables you to shrink locally managed temporary tablespaces and release unused space. You use the SHRINK SPACE clause of the ALTER TABLESPACE statement to shrink a temporary tablespace, or the SHRINK TEMPFILE clause of the ALTER TABLESPACE statement to shrink a single file of a temporary tablespace. Shrinking frees the maximum space possible while maintaining the other attributes of the tablespace or tempfile. The optional KEEP clause defines a minimum size for the tablespace or tempfile.

```
ALTER TABLESPACE temp_ts1 SHRINK SPACE KEEP 30M;
```

DBA_TEMP_FREE_SPACE

The DBA_TEMP_FREE_SPACE dictionary view is new with Oracle 11G. It contains information about space usage for each temporary tablespace. The information includes the space allocated and the free space. You can query this view for these statistics using the following command.

```
SELECT * from DBA_TEMP_FREE_SPACE;
```

Global Temporary Tables

Prior to Oracle 11g, it was not possible to specify a tablespace when creating a global temporary table. In 11G, it is now possible to set the tablespace where the global temporary table will be created. If not specified, the temporary table will be created in the default temporary tablespace. This feature allows you to assign temporary tables to tablespaces with extent sizes appropriate for the use of that table. This, in turn, can lead to improved performance.

SQL Performance Analyzer

Overview of SQL Performance Analyzer

What SPA does

Changes to your database, whether major (such as an upgrade of the Oracle version), or minor (like adding an index) are likely to cause changes to SQL execution plans. While the hope is that these will cause a performance improvement, in some cases, the system changes may cause performance degradation. SQL Performance Analyzer is a tool that can accurately forecast the potential impact of system changes on SQL performance. By doing so, it allows you to tune the system beforehand, in cases where SQL statements regress. If the performance of SQL statements will improve, verifying that ahead of time is also valuable information. SQL Performance Analyzer automates the process of assessing the impact of a change on the SQL workload. It identifies performance divergence for each SQL statement and provides a report that shows the net impact of the change on the workload performance. For regressed SQL statements, it provides execution plan details along with tuning recommendations.

SQL Performance Analyzer can be run on a production database or a test database that closely resembles it. Performing the test on the production system will impact its throughput because SQL Performance Analyzer must execute the SQL statements being tested. Changes made to the system for the test may also affect the database users. Testing major changes, such as a database upgrade, using a production system is not recommended. For changes of that magnitude, you should run SQL Performance Analyzer on a separate test system so that you don't impact the production system.

For the test, be sure that you understand the difference between the **SQL Performance Analyzer** and the **SQL Tuning Advisor**. The SQL Performance Analyzer is designed to help determine the impact of system changes to SQL performance. The SQL Tuning Advisor is designed to help tune SQL in the system as it currently exists.

Sources of SQL statements

Before running the SQL Performance Analyzer, you must capture the SQL statements from the production system that you intend to analyze. Capturing a SQL workload has a negligible performance impact on a production system. Capturing a workload that contains large number SQL statements will better represent the production system database. This will assist SQL Performance Analyzer in accurately forecasting the potential impact of system changes. Ideally, you should capture all SQL statements that are either called by the application or are running on the production database. Captured SQL statements can be stored in a SQL tuning set and used as an input for SQL Performance Analyzer. A SQL tuning set is a database object that includes one or more SQL statements, along with their execution statistics and execution context.

SQL statements can be loaded into a SQL tuning set from many different sources. It's possible to use the cursor cache, Automatic Workload Repository (AWR), or existing SQL tuning sets. Using a SQL tuning set enables you to:

- Store the SQL text and any necessary auxiliary information in a single, persistent database object
- Populate, update, delete, and select captured SQL statements in the SQL tuning set
- Load and merge content from various data sources, such as the Automatic Workload Repository (AWR) or the cursor cache
- Export the SQL tuning set from the system where the SQL workload is captured and import it into another system
- Reuse the SQL workload as an input source for other advisors, such as the SQL Tuning Advisor and the SQL Access Advisor

Views

The following views allow you to monitor SQL Performance Analyzer and view its analysis results:

- The **DBA_ADVISOR_TASKS** view displays descriptive information about the SQL Performance Analyzer task that was created.
- The **DBA_ADVISOR_EXECUTIONS** view displays information about task executions.
- The **DBA_ADVISOR_FINDINGS** view displays the SQL Performance Analyzer findings. SQL Performance Analyzer generates the following types of findings:
    - ✓ Problems, such as performance regression
    - ✓ Symptoms, such as when the structure of an execution plan has changed
    - ✓ Errors, such as nonexistence of an object or view
    - ✓ Informative messages
- The **DBA_ADVISOR_SQLPLANS** view displays a list of all execution plans.
- The **DBA_ADVISOR_SQLSTATS** view displays a list of all SQL compilations and execution statistics.
- The **V$ADVISOR_PROGRESS** view displays the operation progress of SQL Performance Analyzer.

Using SQL Performance Analyzer

Steps in analyzing performance changes

1. Capture the SQL workload that you intend to analyze and store it in a SQL tuning set.
2. If you plan to use a test system separate from your production system, then perform the following steps:
    - ✓ Set up the test system to match the production environment as closely as possible.
    - ✓ Transport the SQL tuning set to the test system.
3. On the test system, create a SQL Performance Analyzer task.
4. Build the pre-change SQL trial by executing the SQL statements stored in the SQL tuning set.
5. Perform the system change.

6. Build the post-change SQL trial by re-executing the SQL statements in the SQL tuning set on the post-change test system.
7. Compare and analyze the pre-change and post-change versions of performance data, and generate a report to identify the SQL statements that have improved, remained unchanged, or regressed after the system change.
8. Tune any regressed SQL statements that are identified.

Processes

Several procedures in the **DBMS_SQLTUNE** package allow you to create, import and export SQL tuning Sets:

- **CREATE_SQLSET** -- creates a SQL tuning set object in the database.
- **LOAD_SQLSET** -- This procedure populates the SQL tuning set with a set of selected SQL. You can call the procedure multiple times to add new SQL statements or replace attributes of existing statements.
- **CREATE_SGTAB_SQLSET** -- This procedure creates a staging table through which SQL Tuning Sets are imported and exported.
- **PACK_STGTAB_SQLSET** -- This procedure copies one or more SQL tuning sets from their location in the SYS schema to a staging table created by the CREATE_STGTAB_SQLSET Procedure.
- **UNPACK_STGTAB_SQLSET** -- This procedure copies one or more SQL tuning sets from their location in the staging table into the SQL tuning sets schema, making them proper SQL tuning sets.

The **DBMS_SQLPA** package contains procedures and functions specific to the SQL Performance Analyzer. These are used to create and execute analyses and report on their findings:

- **CREATE_ANALYSIS_TASK** -- You can use different forms of this function to create analysis tasks for: a single SQL statement from various sources (the SQL text, the AWR, or the cursor cache) or for a SQL tuning set.

- **EXECUTE_ANALYSIS_TASK** -- This function and procedure executes a previously created analysis task, the function version returning the new execution name.

- **REPORT_ANALYSIS_TASK** -- This procedure displays the results of an analysis task.

SQL Plan Management

SQL Plan Baseline Architecture

How SQL Plan Baselines work

Oracle's SQL plan management is intended to prevent performance regressions resulting from sudden changes to the execution plan of a SQL statement. It does so by providing components for capturing, selecting, and evolving SQL plan information. SQL Plan execution can be affected by various changes, such as changes to the optimizer version, statistics, schema, system settings or the application of SQL profiles. Some events, such as dropping an index, can cause irreversible changes to an execution plan. Any number of events can cause regressions in SQL performance, and fixing them can be difficult and time consuming. The SQL Tuning Advisor generates SQL profiles designed to help the optimizer produce well-tuned plans. However, this is a reactive mechanism and can only resolve performance issues after they have occurred and are identified. SQL plan management is a preventative mechanism that records and evaluates the execution plans of SQL statements over time. It builds SQL plan baselines composed of execution plans known to be efficient. The baselines are used to preserve performance of SQL statements, regardless of changes that occur in the system.

SYSAUX Tablespace

The SQL management base (SMB) is a part of the data dictionary and resides in the SYSAUX tablespace. SMB stores statement log, plan histories, SQL plan baselines, and SQL profiles. The SMB is configured with automatic space management enabled which enables weekly purging of unused plans and logs. Because the SMB is stored entirely within the SYSAUX tablespace, SQL plan management and SQL tuning features will not be used if SYSAUX is not available. The SQL Management base will use a set percentage of the SYSAUX tablespace. By default, the

SMB will use no more than 10% of the SYSAUX tablespace. You can set this range between 1% and 50%. A weekly background process measures the total space occupied by the SMB, and will generate a warning in the alert log when the defined limit is exceeded. The alerts continue to be generated weekly until the SMB space limit is increased, the size of the SYSAUX tablespace is increased, or the disk space used by the SMB is decreased. You can change the percentage limit, with the CONFIGURE procedure of the DBMS_SPM package:

```
DBMS_SPM.CONFIGURE('space_budget_percent',30);
```

Weekly, a scheduled purging task manages the disk space used by SQL plan management. The task runs as an automated task in the maintenance window. It will purge any plan that has not been used for more than 53 weeks. Unused plans are identified by the LAST_EXECUTED timestamp stored in the SMB for that plan. The unused plan retention period can range between 5 weeks and 523 weeks. You can use the DBMS_SPM.CONFIGURE procedure to configure the retention period:

```
DBMS_SPM.CONFIGURE('plan_retention_weeks',105);
```

The current configuration settings for the SQL management base can be viewed using the DBA_SQL_MANAGEMENT_CONFIG view:

```
SELECT parameter_name, parameter_value
FROM   dba_sql_management_config;

PARAMETER_NAME              PARAMETER_VALUE
------------------------    ---------------
SPACE_BUDGET_PERCENT                     30
PLAN_RETENTION_WEEKS                    105
```

Set up SQL Plan Baseline

Automatic Plan Capture

Oracle will automatically create and maintain the plan history for SQL statements using information provided by the optimizer when automatic plan capture is enabled. The plan history will include information required by the optimizer to reproduce an execution plan. This includes the SQL text, outline, bind variables, and compilation environment. The first time a plan is generated for a given SQL statement, that plan is marked as accepted for use by the optimizer. That initial plan represents both the plan history and the SQL plan baseline. Any subsequent plans for that SQL statement will be included in the plan history. Any of these later plans that are verified not to cause performance regressions will be added to the SQL plan baseline during the SQL plan baseline evolution phase. The initialization parameter OPTIMIZER_CAPTURE_SQL_PLAN_BASELINES must be set to TRUE to enable automatic plan capture. By default, this parameter is set to FALSE.

Loading Plans Manually

It's also possible to manually create SQL plan baselines. You do this by loading existing plans for a set of SQL statements as SQL plan baselines. The manually loaded plans are not verified for performance, but are added as accepted plans immediately. You can use manual plan loading by itself, or in addition to automatic plan capture. You can load plans from SQL Tuning Sets and AWR Snapshots, or the Cursor Cache.

- **DBMS_SPM.LOAD_PLANS_FROM_SQLSET** -- Allows you to load plans from a SQL Tuning Set. To load plans from Automatic Workload Repository (AWR), you must first load the plans stored in AWR snapshots into a SQL Tuning Set using the CREATE_SQLSET and LOAD_SQLSET procedures.
- **DBMS_SPM.LOAD_PLANS_FROM_CURSOR_CACHE** -- Allows you to load plans from the cursor cache.

Using SQL Plan Baseline

Selecting SQL Plan Baselines

When selecting from stored baseline plans for a given SQL statement, the Oracle database detects plan changes based on the stored plan history. It will select a plan to avoid potential performance regression for a given statement. Whenever a SQL statement is compiled, the optimizer initially uses a cost-based search to build a best-cost plan. It will then try to locate a match in the SQL plan baseline. If one is found, the optimizer will make use of the matching plan. If no match is found, it evaluates the cost of each accepted plan in the SQL plan baseline and uses the plan with the lowest cost. If the best-cost plan generated by the optimizer does not match any plans in the plan history for the SQL statement, it is added as a non-accepted plan to the plan history. The new plan will not be used until it is verified to not cause a performance regression. If a change in the system (such as a dropped index) causes all accepted plans to become non-reproducible, the optimizer will select the best-cost plan without regard to its acceptance status. To enable the use of SQL plan baselines, you must set the OPTIMIZER_USE_SQL_PLAN_BASELINES initialization parameter to TRUE (default).

Evolving SQL Plan Baselines

In order for new plans in the SQL plan history to be used, they must be accepted. Acceptance of SQL Plans occurs during the SQL Plan baseline evolution phase. During this phase, the database evaluates the performance of new plans and integrates the best plans into SQL plan baselines. When a non-accepted plan is verified to not cause a performance regression, it is changed to an accepted plan and integrated into the SQL plan baseline. A successful verification of a non-accepted plan consists of comparing it to an accepted plan in the SQL plan baseline and ensuring the new plan delivers better performance. Existing SQL plan baselines can be evolved by manually loading plans either from the cursor cache or from a SQL tuning set. Manually load plans are automatically added as accepted plans. The PL/SQL function DBMS_SPM.EVOLVE_SQL_PLAN_BASELINE attempts to evolve new plans added by the optimizer to the SQL plan history. If EVOLVE_SQL_PLAN_BASELINE can verify that the new plan performs better than an accepted plan chosen from the corresponding SQL plan baseline, it is added as an accepted plan.

Fixed Plans

A SQL plan baseline is defined as 'fixed' if it contains at least one enabled plan that has the FIXED attribute set to YES. Fixed SQL plan baselines are used to limit the set of possible plans (usually one plan) for a SQL statement. They can also be used to migrate an existing stored outline by loading the "outlined" plan as a fixed plan. When a fixed SQL plan baseline also contains non-fixed plans, the optimizer gives preference to fixed plans over non-fixed ones. The optimizer will pick the fixed plan with the least cost over a non-fixed plan with an even lower cost. Only if none of the fixed plans is reproducible, will the optimizer will pick a non-fixed plan. The optimizer will not automatically add new plans to a fixed SQL plan baseline. Because new plans are not automatically added, DBMS_SPM.EVOLVE_SQL_PLAN_BASELINE does not evolve a fixed SQL plan baseline. A fixed SQL plan baseline can only be evolved by manually loading new plans into it. If the SQL Tuning Advisor creates a profile for a SQL statement with a fixed SQL plan baseline, by default that profile won't be used. The tuned plan is added to the fixed SQL plan baseline as a non-fixed plan. Since non-fixed plans aren't used except by necessity when a SQL Plan is fixed, in order for the tuned plan to be utilized, you must manually alter the tuned plan to a fixed plan by setting its FIXED attribute to YES.

Displaying SQL Plan Baselines

You can view the plans stored in the SQL plan baseline for a given statement by using the DISPLAY_SQL_PLAN_BASELINE function of the DBMS_XPLAN package. This function displays one or more execution plans for the specified SQL statement, specified by the **sql_handle**. You can display a single plan by supplying a plan name. The function uses plan information stored in the SQL management base to explain and display the plans.

```
SELECT *
FROM    table(dbms_xplan.display_sql_plan_baseline(
                sql_handle  => 'SYS_SQL_109c10fabeeec639',
                format      => 'basic')
         );
```

Automatic SQL Tuning

In 11G, the SQL tuning process has been improved with the addition of automatic SQL tuning features. These automatic tuning process has been designed to work equally well for OLTP databases. The automated tuning process is implemented by four functions in the Oracle database:

- Automatic Database Diagnostic Monitor (ADDM)
- SQL Tuning Advisor
- SQL Tuning Sets
- SQL Access Advisor

The Automatic Database Diagnostic Monitor (ADDM) analyzes the information collected by the AWR for possible performance problems. High-load SQL statements identified by ADDM become targets for tuning by the SQL Tuning Advisor. SQL Tuning Advisor is designed to optimize the performance of SQL statements. By default, Oracle Database automatically identifies implements tuning recommendations for problematic SQL statements using the SQL Tuning Advisor during system maintenance windows as an automated maintenance task. During the window, it searches for ways to improve the execution plans of the high-load SQL statements. The SQL Tuning Advisor can also be run manually at any time on any given SQL workload to improve performance. If multiple SQL statements are used as input to ADDM, SQL Tuning Advisor, or SQL Access Advisor, a SQL Tuning Set (STS) is constructed and stored. A SQL Tuning Set includes the SQL statements along with their associated execution context and basic execution statistics. A companion process to the SQL Tuning Advisor, the SQL Access Advisor provides advice on materialized views, indexes, and materialized view logs. It's designed to improve performance by recommending the ideal set of materialized views, materialized view logs, and indexes for a given workload. As a rule of thumb, increasing the number of and space allocated to materialized views and indexes improves query performance. The SQL Access Advisor considers the trade-offs between space usage and query performance. It works to recommend the most cost-effective configuration of new and existing materialized views and indexes.

Automatic Tuning Optimizer

As SQL statements are executed by the Oracle database, the query optimizer works to generate good execution plans for them. The query optimizer has two modes of operation: a normal mode and a tuning mode. When using normal mode, the optimizer compiles the SQL and generates an execution plan with sub-second time constraints during which it must find a good execution plan. When running in tuning mode, the optimizer performs additional analysis to check whether 'normal' execution plan can be improved upon. The output of the query optimizer in tuning mode is not an execution plan. Rather it create a series of actions, along with a rationale and expected benefit for producing a significantly superior plan. When running in the tuning mode, the optimizer is referred to as the Automatic Tuning Optimizer. While running in tuning mode, the optimizer can take several minutes to tune a single statement. It's not practical to invoke the Automatic Tuning Optimizer every time a query has to be hard-parsed. It is meant to be used for complex and high-load SQL statements that have a negative impact on the database. The Automatic Tuning Optimizer performs four types of tuning analysis.

Statistics Analysis

Oracle's query optimizer makes use of object statistics to generate execution plans. When statistics are stale or missing, the optimizer can generate sub-optimal execution plans. The Automatic Tuning Optimizer checks for missing or stale statistics, and produces two types of output. The first is recommendations to gather statistics for objects where the statistics are stale or missing. The second type of statistics output is auxiliary information. This takes the form of statistics for objects with no statistics, and statistic adjustment factor for objects with stale statistics. This auxiliary information is stored in an object called a SQL Profile.

SQL Profiling

Sometimes the query optimizer produces inaccurate estimates about an attribute of a statement due to lack of information, leading to poor execution plans. This can sometimes be corrected by manually adding hints to the SQL in order to guide the optimizer into making better decisions. Hints are not always effective, are labor intensive, and are often impractical when using packaged applications. SQL profiling is intended to be a solution for this problem. The Automatic Tuning Optimizer stores additional data regarding the SQL statement called a SQL Profile. The profile consists of auxiliary statistics specific to that statement. A SQL Profile collects additional information using sampling and partial execution techniques to help the optimizer make decisions about cardinality and other traits of the SQL query. In addition, the Automatic Tuning Optimizer also uses execution history information of the SQL statement to appropriately set optimizer parameter settings in the profile. An accepted SQL Profile is stored persistently in the data dictionary. SQL Profile's are specific to the particular query they were created for. After accepting the profile, if that statement is executed in the database again, the optimizer uses normal statistics in addition to the profile data when generating an execution plan. The additional information makes it possible to produce well-tuned plans for the corresponding SQL statement without. A SQL Profile does not act like a stored outline to freeze the execution plan of a SQL statement. As changes happen to the tables against which the SQL is run, the execution plan can change with the same SQL Profile.

Access Path Analysis

The use of indexes can tremendously enhance performance of a SQL statement. Properly used, they can reduce the need for full table scans on large tables and speed up join operations when querying multiple tables. Adding indexes to tables is a common method to drop query times. One of the functions of the Automatic Tuning Optimizer is to investigate whether a new index can significantly enhance the performance of a query. If it identifies the need for such an index, it recommends its creation. The Automatic Tuning Optimizer does not analyze how its index recommendation can affect the remainder of the SQL workload. It therefore also recommends running the SQL Access Advisor utility on the SQL statement along with a representative SQL workload. Unlike the Automatic Tuning Advisor, the SQL Access Advisor does look at the impact of creating an index on the entire SQL workload before making any recommendations.

SQL Structure Analysis

The Automatic Tuning Optimizer identifies common problems with the structure of SQL statements that can lead to poor performance. The structure issues could be syntactic, semantic, or design problems with the statement. Whatever the issue, Automatic Tuning Optimizer makes relevant suggestions to restructure the SQL statements. It will suggest an alternative that is similar, but not equivalent, to the original statement. For example, the optimizer may suggest replacing a UNION operator with a UNION ALL or to replace NOT IN with NOT EXISTS. The developer can then decide if the advice is applicable in the given situation. SQL structure changes require a deep understanding of the data properties and should be implemented only after considering all the implications.

Automatic SQL Tuning

The SQL Tuning Advisor runs as an automated task on high-load SQL statements identified by the AWR as tuning candidates. This task, called Automatic SQL Tuning, runs in the default maintenance windows on a nightly basis. By default, it will run for at most one hour during any given maintenance window and perform the following steps:

- **Identify SQL candidates in the AWR for tuning.** Oracle uses data from the AWR to generate a list of potential SQL statements that are eligible for tuning. Candidates will typically be repeating high-load statements that have a significant impact on the system. Only statements that have an execution plan with a high potential for improvement will be marked for tuning. Recursive SQL and statements that have been tuned recently are ignored, as are parallel queries, DMLs, AND DDLs. The candidates are then ordered based on their performance impact. The performance impact of a SQL statement is calculated by summing the CPU time and the I/O times captured in the AWR for that SQL statement in the past week.
- **Each SQL statement is individually tuned by calling the SQL Tuning Advisor.** During the tuning process, all recommendation types are considered and reported, but only SQL profiles can be implemented automatically.

- **Test SQL profiles by executing the SQL statement.** If a SQL profile is recommended, the tuning advisor will execute the SQL statement with and without the profile.
- **Optionally implement the SQL profiles.** Only if the performance improvement improves at least threefold, the SQL profile will be accepted automatically (and only if the ACCEPT_SQL_PROFILES task parameter is set to TRUE). A profile will not be implemented if the objects referenced in the SQL statement have stale optimizer statistics. SQL profiles that have been implemented automatically will have their type set to AUTO in the DBA_SQL_PROFILES view.

Setup and modify Automatic SQL Tuning

Configuring Automatic SQL Tuning

The behavior of the automatic SQL tuning task can be configured using the DBMS_SQLTUNE package. In order to use the APIs, the user needs to be granted at least the ADVISOR privilege. DBMS_SQLTUNE allows you to configure the standard behavior of the SQL Tuning Advisor, as well as configuring automatic SQL tuning. You do so by specifying the task parameters using the SET_TUNING_TASK_PARAMETER procedure. Because the automatic tuning task is owned by SYS, only the SYS user can set the task parameters for it.

```
BEGIN
  DBMS_SQLTUNE.SET_TUNING_TASK_PARAMETER(
          task_name  => 'SYS_AUTO_SQL_TUNING_TASK',
          parameter  => 'ACCEPT_SQL_PROFILES', value =>
'TRUE');
END;
```

- **ACCEPT_SQL_PROFILE** -- Specifies whether to accept SQL profiles automatically.
- **MAX_SQL_PROFILES_PER_EXEC** -- Specifies the limit of SQL profiles that are accepted for each automatic SQL tuning task.
- **MAX_AUTO_SQL_PROFILES** -- Specifies the limit of SQL profiles that are accepted in total.
- **EXECUTION_DAYS_TO_EXPIRE** -- Specifies the number of days for which to save the task history in the advisor framework schema. By default, the task history is saved for 30 days.

Viewing Automatic SQL Tuning Reports

You can use the **DBMS_SQLTUNE.REPORT_AUTO_TUNING_TASK** function to generate an automatic SQL tuning report. The report contains information about all executions of the automatic SQL tuning task. In order to run this report, you need the ADVISOR privilege and SELECT privileges on the DBA_ADVISOR views. The standard SQL tuning report generated using the DBMS_SQLTUNE.REPORT_TUNING_TASK function, contains information about a single task execution of the SQL Tuning Advisor. By contrast, the automatic SQL tuning report contains information about multiple executions of the automatic SQL tuning task. Depending on the sections that are included in a report, you can view the following information about the automatic SQL tuning task:

- **General information** -- provides a high-level description of the automatic SQL tuning task. It includes information about the inputs given for the report, the number of SQL statements tuned during the maintenance, and the number of SQL profiles that were created
- **Summary** -- lists the SQL statements that were tuned during the maintenance window and the estimated benefit of each SQL profile, or their actual execution statistics after test executing the SQL statement with the SQL profile
- **Tuning findings** -- contains the following information about each SQL statement analyzed by the SQL Tuning Advisor:

- ✓ All findings associated with each SQL statement
- ✓ Whether the profile was accepted on the system, and why
- ✓ Whether the SQL profile is currently enabled on the system
- ✓ Detailed execution statistics captured when testing the SQL profile
- **Explain plans** -- shows the old and new explain plans used by each SQL statement analyzed by the SQL Tuning Advisor.
- **Errors** -- lists all errors encountered by the automatic SQL tuning task.

SQL Tuning Information Views

- **DBA_ADVISOR_ACTIONS** -- displays information about the actions associated with all recommendations in the database.
- **DBA_ADVISOR_TASKS** -- displays information about all tasks in the database.
- **DBA_ADVISOR_EXECUTIONS** -- displays metadata information for task executions.
- **DBA_ADVISOR_FINDINGS** -- displays the findings discovered by all advisors in the database.
- **DBA_ADVISOR_RECOMMENDATIONS** -- displays the results of an analysis of all recommendations in the database.
- **DBA_ADVISOR_RATIONALE** -- displays information about the rationales for all recommendations in the database.
- **DBA_ADVISOR_SQLSTATS** -- displays execution statistics for the test-execution of different SQL plans during the advisor analysis.
- **DBA_ADVISOR_SQLPLANS** -- displays the different SQL execution plans generated as part of an advisor analysis.

ABOUT THE AUTHOR

Matthew Morris is an Oracle Database Administrator and Developer currently employed as a Database Engineer with Computer Sciences Corporation. Matthew has worked with the Oracle database since 1996 when he worked in the RDBMS support team for Oracle Support Services. Employed with Oracle for over eleven years in support and development positions, Matthew was an early adopter of the Oracle Certified Professional program. He was one of the first one hundred Oracle Certified Database Administrators (version 7.3) and in the first hundred to become an Oracle Certified Forms Developer. In the years since, he has upgraded his Database Administrator certification for releases 8i, 9i, 10G and 11G, and added the Application Express Expert certification. Outside of Oracle, he has CompTIA certifications in Linux+ and Security+.

Made in the USA
Middletown, DE
05 December 2015